Dyslexia is Not a Disease—
It's a Learning Difference

Dyslexia is Not a Disease— It's a Learning Difference

THEORETICAL AND PRACTICAL APPROACHES TO TEACHING STRUGGLING READERS WITH LEARNING DIFFERENCES

Mamie B. Crockett Ph.D.

Walter L. Crockett Ph.D.

Copyright © 2015 Mamie B. Crockett, PhD, Walter L. Crockett, PhD, and Jeton McClinton, PhD
All rights reserved.

ISBN: 1503397580
ISBN 13: 9781503397583
Library of Congress Control Number: 2015902350
CreateSpace Independent Publishing Platform
North Charleston, South Carolina

About the Authors

Mamie B. Crockett is the cofounder and executive director of the Learning Tree Academic and Community Development Center. She received a Master of Arts in Teaching, with a cognate in English Education, from Manhattanville College of the Sacred Heart. Her terminal degree is in educational leadership, with a cognate in literacy. Certified in remedial reading, language arts, and social studies, she has taught students from kindergarten to the graduate level. During her professional career, she has served as an instructional specialist at a large, urban school district and conducted professional development sessions for elementary-level classroom teachers. For ten-plus years, she trained teachers how to identify and implement effective instructional strategies for students with characteristics of dyslexia. She also presented frequently at state, regional, and national professional conferences, with lectures such as "Helping the Late Bloomer" and "Dyslexia Is Not a Disease." These talks inspired a tremendous amount of positive feedback, and resulted in the writing of this book.

Walter L. Crockett is a visiting professor and associate director with the Executive PhD Program at Jackson State University. He received a Doctor of Philosophy degree from Ohio State University in the field of educational research and development, with a cognate in counseling psychology. His professional career has been at the university level, where he served in a variety of academic and administration positions, which included director of psychometric services; chair of the Department of School, Community and Rehabilitation Counseling, and associate dean of the School of Administrative Leadership. He is an editor and published author and has conducted research in the areas of student motivation and academic performance. He is currently piloting for publication a brief counseling model designed for middle-school males in an urban setting. This counseling model is designed to motivate middle-school males to display positive behaviors and attitudes that will enhance their academic success. He is a

National Board Certified Counselor Educator and has completed the Harvard Institute for School Leadership Program. He currently serves as an academic advisor and dissertation chair to doctoral students pursuing a degree in Urban Higher Education.

About The Editors

Joyce Dennetta Brown Harris is a reading specialist and educational consultant who provides editorial, external evaluation, and professional and curriculum development services for educational agencies. She has a Master of Science degree in reading and received a Doctorate of Education in supervision and curriculum development from the University of Alabama–Tuscaloosa. She has served in the capacities of professor of reading, associate dean, interim dean of education, and director of the Harris/Gambrell Reading Center, named in her honor, at Jackson State University. She has been a member of the Board of Examiners (BOE) for the National Council for Accreditation of Teacher Education and provided extensive services as a consultant to various schools and educational organizations. She has provided training in the Parents as Teachers Program at the Mississippi Learning Institute and an initiative for fathers in the Picayune Head Start program. She has authored and implemented the Family Circle for Learning Project, a parent/child/teacher initiative of Mississippi Action for Progress.

Tracy Harris is an associate professor in the Department of Elementary and Early Childhood Education at Jackson State University. She holds a doctorate in early childhood education, with a cognate in reading, is a specialist in psychometry, and has a Master of Public Administration in organizational management. She serves as director of the Harris-Gambrell Reading Center, which provides assessments and interventions for struggling readers. She is also a psychometrist and works in partnership with the Departments of Communicative Disorders and Special Education on projects that promote collaborative clinical experiences for elementary education, special education, and speech and language pathology students. She is a program reviewer for the International Literacy Association and holds a current Mississippi Educator License in nursery–grade one, elementary education, English, psychometry, and remedial reading (K–12). She has served as a faculty mentor for a Ronald E. McNair scholar and was awarded a grant from the Center for Undergraduate Research in which she trained four undergraduate students, and supervised and developed their research project.

Jeton McClinton is an associate professor in the Department of Educational Leadership at Jackson State University. She received the Doctor of Philosophy degree from Mississippi State University and a Master of Arts in educational technology from George Washington University. She has more than fifteen years of experience in instructional technology, visual and digital literacy, and distance education design and delivery, with extensive experience in e-learning systems methodologies. She has designed and provided technical training and support, serving the needs of faculty, students, and administrators. She serves as an editor and reviewer of numerous local, national, and international journals. She has published more than fifty peer-reviewed conference proceedings, monographs, journal articles, and book chapters on electronic portfolios, instructional technology, distance learning, digital technologies, and faculty development.

Preface

In act 5 of *Macbeth*, Shakespeare wrote some piercing lines that have caused some educators to reflect on their efforts to make a difference: "Life is but a walking shadow, a poor player that struts and frets his hour upon the stage, and then is heard no more; it is a tale told by an idiot, full of sound and fury, signifying nothing." As educators, we do not want our "hour upon the stage" in education to be full of sound and fury—renaming old theories and leaving students wanting. To profoundly struggling readers, such stale efforts ultimately *signify nothing*.

We have spent thousands of hours in classrooms, observed teacher and student dialogue, and recorded some of the best practices of teachers in the profession. This book is designed to assist the sincere teacher, school administrator, or parent who wants to help a struggling reader but may not know what to do or where to start. It will not provide all the answers or present all the best strategies that work; however, we have made a concerted effort to present examples of unique learning differences that describe, in particular, a dyslexic learner in ways that will enable a reader to say, "Aha, so that could be Johnny's reading disability."

This book primarily addresses the needs of struggling readers with characteristics of dyslexia. It proposes to enlighten educators on all levels so that they will be able to identify unique learning differences that may require accommodations that are more therapeutic than traditional classroom interventions. To do this, chapter 1 defines, describes, and identifies common characteristics of dyslexia. Chapters 2 and 3 present further discussions on learning and reading styles that may be influenced by related behavioral disabilities. Chapter 4 describes the various learning behaviors: auditory-linguistic, visual-spatial, and a combination of auditory-linguistic and visual-spatial behaviors. Using several operational definitions, various aspects of this language-based disorder are addressed in chapters 5 and 6, where suggested instructional strategies are matched with learning styles, ranging from A to Z.

Essentially, dyslexia is discussed and presented as a neurological brain difference that affects millions, usually one in five. It is a specific language-based disability that can affect a person's ability to read, write, spell, and sometimes speak. Society in general cannot afford to neglect the approximately 20 percent of the school population that has mild to profound characteristics of dyslexia. It is estimated that the majority of school dropouts are struggling dyslexic learners who gave up.

In chapter 7, concerted effort is given to spelling and the reciprocal skills of reading and writing. It is imperative to emphasize the basic need for sound/print connections when teaching the dyslexic reader. Like most other struggling readers, dyslexic students usually (a) have low phonemic awareness and letter recognition; (b) lack phonics knowledge and the ability to apply sounds; (c) lack fluency in reading; (d) may verbalize words but lack comprehension; and (e) lack skills in writing and spelling but may have a relatively large oral vocabulary with applicable connections to life experiences.

In chapter 8, some avenues are proposed from the perspective of the global-learning community. School reform is addressed in light of *who is still left behind*. The results of some case studies appear in chapter 9 along with a discussion of action research projects that were designed to help synthesize the different aspects that need to be considered for the struggling dyslexic reader. A brief discussion is included on related learning styles and behaviors that may resemble characteristics of dyslexia and common strategies that can be adapted.

Some inclusive perspectives are also expressed by other writers (Caine, Caine, McClintic, and Klimek 2009; Jensen 2000). Because dyslexic tendencies are so widespread, it seems most practical to broaden the base to struggling readers in general and not those peculiar to one kind of learner. Even though many agree that others with mild or minimal reading difficulties will benefit from multisensory instruction, it is emphasized here that the person who possesses profound characteristics of dyslexia needs intense therapeutic instruction in order to change the brain so that learning can take place in a timely manner. To further support and accommodate struggling readers, the final section also contains a glossary of terms and special resources with websites, online resources, and cutting-edge technology that can assist school administrators in providing affordable educational services for all kinds of learners without fear of reprisal.

Purpose

The purpose of this book is to help struggling readers with characteristics of dyslexia and related learning differences. For educators, school administrators, and stakeholders, this book provides some solutions based on research studies of the brain that relate to learning. By providing a better understanding of the kinds of learners served and inexpensive strategies and resources that can be used to assist children during the early and middle years, this book supports parents as well as teachers. The references and resources provided will also help homeschooling parents make informed decisions.

We encourage school leaders to study the educational programs selected to ensure that they include the principles of Dr. Samuel Orton (neurologist) and Anna Gillingham (educator at the Neurological Institute of New York) who initiated the therapeutic and multisensory (kinesthetic) strategies for teaching those with dyslexia. They pioneered the process of engaging multiple senses in the learning process, a strategy that is recommended for different learners by most research-based programs used by the Orton Dyslexia Society (Liuzzo 2008).

After developing and administering a checklist designed to identify these multisensory learning differences of students, approximately 250 teachers over a five-year period provided anecdotal data and test scores that indicated more research and support were needed. It became clear that more should be done to support teachers in this quest to solve learning issues of students at minimum cost. To do this, selected teachers and interested colleagues collaborated in piloting a dyslexia program, the Dyslexia Training Program at the Texas Scottish Rite Hospital for Children, and supplementary programs (e.g., READ 180) to help struggling readers. Follow-up data from teachers, principals, college professors, parents, and struggling learners laid the groundwork for much of the collaboration and instructional designs included in this book. Our purpose is to provide teachers with accommodating strategies for struggling readers so that they can help these students succeed in the regular classroom.

Table of Contents

About the Authors		v
About The Editors		vii
Preface		ix
Purpose		xi
Chapter 1	**Characteristics of Dyslexia**	1
	The Learning Style Called Dyslexia	4
	Brain-Compatible Learning Environments	8
	Perspectives of School Administrators	10
Chapter 2	**Different Reading Styles and Environmental Factors**	14
	The Dyslexic Reading Style and Related Reading Difficulties	16
	The Learning-Different Student	19
	Dyslexia: Nature or Nurture?	21
	Impoverished Environments and Educational Risk Factors	28
Chapter 3	**The Educational Environment and Behavioral Issues**	33
	Organizing the Environment	34
	Strategies for Bonding with Students	38
	Dyslexia, ADD, and Related Behavioral and Learning Differences	39
	Checklist for Setting up a Brain-Compatible Learning Environment	44

| Chapter 4 | **Literacy Screening Designed for Enhanced Instruction** | 47 |

Identifying Reading Styles and
Addressing Reading Difficulties — 48
Selected Best Practices and Strategies — 55

| Chapter 5 | **Learning Styles and Concomitant Instructional Strategies** | 58 |

Student Learning Styles and Suggested
Instructional Strategies — 59
Differentiating Instruction and Accommodating
Learning Differences — 65
Modifying Instruction for Hard-to-Reach Students
with Reading Difficultie — 67
Universal Instructional Strategies for Different Learners — 71

| Chapter 6 | **Instructional Spelling Strategies to Enhance Reading and Writing** | 74 |

The Reciprocal Skills of Reading and Writing — 77
Connecting the Five Components of Reading — 82
The Decoding Spelling Continuum with
Grade-Level Expectations — 87
Traditional Best Practices: Revisited — 94

| Chapter 7 | **Accountability and Support for Different Learners** | 99 |

Accountability of School Administrators — 100
Accountability of Teachers — 101
Instructional Accountability: A-to-Z Teaching Styles and
Strategies for Different Learners — 102
Accountability and Classroom Paraprofessionals — 106
Classroom Management and Accountability — 107

| Chapter 8 | **School Reform and the Evolving Modern Classroom** | 110 |

School Reform: Where Do We Go from Here? — 111
Literacy: The Root of Academic Success — 114
Addressing Diversity in the Classroom — 116
Literacy Strategies for Struggling Diverse Learners — 117

Chapter 9	**Action Research: Techniques to Help Teachers Instruct Students with Dyslexia**	**128**
	Case Reports	130
	Problem-Based Learning and Action Research	133
	Action Research: Standards-Based Project	134

Resource Section — 139

Glossary of Select Terms — 159

Selected Bibliography — 162

Subject Index Page — 185

CHAPTER 1
Characteristics of Dyslexia

Chapter Subheadings
The Learning Style Called Dyslexia
Brain-Compatible Learning Environments
Perspectives of School Administrators

OBJECTIVE
To present dyslexia as a difference in learning style that is connected with key functions of the brain.

TERMS TO KNOW
Brain-compatible learning environments: environments that empower learners, developed through observing key principles of the brain and associated learning processes.

Dyslexia: a learning difference caused by inherited neurological brain functions that affect the way one perceives language (visual, auditory, spatial, and linguistic).

Tier 1: quality classroom instruction based on a standard curriculum framework.

Tier 2: supplemental instruction that focuses on conceptual gaps assessed in Tier 1.

Tier 3: intensive interventions (usually thirty minutes to one hour daily) specifically designed to meet the individual needs of students who did not succeed in Tiers 1 and 2.

Reading disability: the inability of a student to read at the same level as his or her peers even though he or she has been exposed to the same quality of instruction.

Remedial instruction: direct systematic instruction for one to three students at a time.

Progress monitoring: an ongoing process assessing a student's performance, measured through informal classroom, benchmark, and large-scale assessments.

Many educators, parents, and even students want to know what dyslexia is, how it affects learning, and what causes it. To respond to these concerns, this chapter addresses dyslexia from the perspective of learning styles and provides some of the latest references and helpful scientific explanations regarding this learning difference. Learning differences are addressed in a general way, but the focus is on presenting dyslexia as a learning difference that is *not* a disease.

When some parents seek (often out of total frustration) to know what is going on with their child, frequently teachers are reluctant to discuss this learning style, even when parents have had the child tested and diagnosed. Some educators seem to respond to the unique difference as if it is a disease that should not be discussed with teachers or with parents. Therefore, effort has been made here to be bold and say that this book is not just about dyslexia—it is about *learning differences*. It is designed to help teachers identify dyslexia from various vantage points so that they will know that one size does not fit all. There are varying degrees of dyslexia—ranging from mild to profound characteristics. For example, one may find characteristics coupled with behavior such as ADD (attention deficit disorder). To address these diverse needs, one has to look at behavioral and cognitive needs. Treating the symptoms is better for the student than ignoring his or her needs or placing an otherwise intelligent student in the lowest reading group.

At this juncture, it should be made clear that this learning difference is caused by unique functions of the brain. Specifically, the brain normally receives and sends messages through the nervous system. The central nervous system is the control center of the body and includes the brain and spinal cord. When the brain relays the message to walk, for example, the body voluntarily proceeds to walk and executes numerous functions controlled by the brain, a grayish-white, rounded, cottage-cheese-like organ located in the skull. The brain serves as the command center of the central nervous system, which consists of at least one hundred billion cells.

Scientists have studied the brain, labeled areas of it, and provided extensive details about those areas. But the focus in this chapter is only on the areas that most directly affect reading, especially the functions of the dyslexic brain.

Over the years, the definition of this learning difference has evolved. On November 12, 2002, the board of directors of the International Dyslexia Association (IDA) collaborated with reading experts who have conducted scientific studies over many years, including those of the National Institute of Child Health and Human Development (NICHD). The IDA adopted the following definition and posted it online as the formal definition of dyslexia:

> Dyslexia is a specific learning disability that is neurobiological in origin. It is characterized by difficulties with accurate and/or fluent word recognition and by poor spelling and decoding abilities. These difficulties typically result from a deficit in the phonological component of language that is often unexpected in relation to other cognitive abilities and the provision of effective classroom instruction. Secondary consequences may include problems in reading comprehension and reduced reading experience that can impede growth of vocabulary and background knowledge. (Lyon, Shaywitz, and Shaywitz, as cited in Moats and Dakin 2008, 4)

To simplify some terms and abbreviate this definition, several modified definitions and descriptions of dyslexia are provided throughout this book to assist readers in understanding the multidimensional characteristics of dyslexia. For example, it may be interesting to trace the origin of the word *dyslexia*. Dyslexia is formed from the Latin *dys*, meaning "difficult," and the Greek word *lexis*, meaning "word" or "speech." By general definition, dyslexia is a language disorder that can affect a person's ability to read, write, spell, and sometimes speak.

Dyslexia is often manifested by various language difficulties generally including reading problems with conspicuously weak skills in writing and spelling. These problems are individually unique—much like fingerprints—appearing in different perceptual configurations. Even though labeling students is not always appropriate, it is helpful and important to understand that dyslexic students are in need of specific academic accommodations.

These different learners know that reading print is a horrendous problem, and the issues are compounded when they are mistakenly put in special-education classes or called "lazy" when they struggle to acquire a basic understanding of the alphabetic principles. Out of frustration, students with characteristics of dyslexia have made such statements as the following:

> *Everyone is reading the assigned passage smoothly except for me. I stumble over almost every word! What's wrong with me? Why am I different? How are the other students able to understand these little squiggles and lines and call them by name?*

The answer is, "You are a different kind of learner."

While most students can master the letters and sounds after a general introduction and practice, dyslexic students need to tactilely relate the alphabetic principles (letters and sounds) of the language with something physical in order to stimulate long-term memory and develop dendrites in the brain. They must be taught the rules connected with the alphabetic code to read effectively and fluently. Indeed, dyslexic students are different, and they share this difference with 20 percent of the general population. This group usually represents about 80 percent of students who have not been diagnosed as having characteristics of dyslexia or a related learning disability. The remaining 20 percent may exhibit mild to profound dyslexic tendencies and are frequently seen as the fringe population—at both ends of the continuum.

A reading disability is indeed a learning disability. It means that individuals with this disability are unable to perform as well as their peers and are unable to read at the expected level even when these individuals are exposed to the same quality of instruction as their peers. Regrettably, students with reading difficulties are sometimes treated as if they have a disease; they are isolated from the general student population and sometimes even "quarantined" behind room dividers.

One writer observed that if illiteracy were truly studied like a disease, it would be scrutinized under a microscope, put through a CAT scan, and dissected by researchers, who would search for a cure and provide immediate feedback to education professionals. Teachers would then be well prepared and would diagnose learning styles and prescribe the appropriate intervention strategies, resources, and services. Students exhibiting characteristics of dyslexia, or a similar disability, would seldom be wrongly labeled or placed in isolation from the general student population as if they had a contagious disease. And school leaders would make morning rounds in the schools to ensure that all students were learning well.

Unfortunately, many teachers have not received adequate training in the area of dyslexia and other reading disabilities and are unable to assist students in developing effective coping and learning strategies. When resources are limited, teachers and administrators often cater to the needs of the mainstream of the student population. These students are often neglected or underserved.

The Learning Style Called Dyslexia

Learning styles is probably the most student-friendly and teacher-friendly term to use when addressing the broad needs of struggling readers. Probably the most profound research on dyslexia done in this decade was conducted by Dr. Sally Shaywitz and her team. These researchers substantiated how dyslexia can affect every aspect of a student's life. In the book *Overcoming Dyslexia* (2003, 4), Shaywitz explained that it is a *hidden* disability.

> It is invisible to the observer, but very evident to those who have it. Acknowledged was that we can no longer ignore the existence of *dyslexia* because people with *dyslexia* "can point to an image of the brain's internal workings, made possible by new brain imagining technology.... [Scientists and educators can observe] exactly where and how *dyslexia* manifests itself in the brain."

It seems that many educators view dyslexia as an "educational disease" to be avoided. If a student performs well in class but poorly on tests, the teacher may often decide that this student simply failed to apply known skills. However, students with characteristics of dyslexia may be able to perform above average in other academic areas—such as in project-based subjects, in math where basic math rules remain constant, or in areas where oral responses are accepted—but perform below average in subjects or tests requiring written-language responses and, as consequence, may be criticized for not achieving at their expected level. For example, if John is passing with a B or above in math or science, he is expected to be at least a C student in reading and language arts; if, instead, he fails the latter, he may be labeled as "lazy." "The student is smart. I expect him to write responses to the story after we finish reading, but he never writes anything that makes sense!" stated one frustrated teacher. In these situations, students who cannot follow through with written responses are commonly labeled as "lazy" or "not trying."

Students who have been diagnosed with dyslexia have described their struggles in different ways. One classic case that comes to mind is described in the autobiography *Thank You, Mr. Falker*, by Patricia Polacco. In this touching book, Trisha, the little girl in the story (who is the author at age ten), describes how her love for reading was fostered by her grandparents who shared the joy of reading:

> *Grandpa held the jar of honey so that all the family could see, then dipped a ladle into it and drizzled honey on the cover of a small book. The little girl had just turned five. "Stand up, little one," he cooed. "I did this for your mother, your uncles, your older brother, and now you!" Then he handed the book to her. "Taste!"*

> *She dipped her finger into the honey and put it into her mouth. "What is that taste?" the grandma asked. The little girl answered, "Sweet!" Then all of the family said in a single voice, "Yes, and so is knowledge, but knowledge is like the bee that made the sweet honey, you have to chase it through the pages of a book."* (Polacco, 16)

Trisha knew that the promise to read was at last hers. Soon she was going to learn to read.

But being read to did not alleviate her need to get help in understanding the alphabetic code. The story reveals how Trisha, a fifth-grader, is mocked and called "dummy" by her classmates for not being able to read fluently: "When Trisha looked at a page, all she saw were wiggling shapes, and when she tried to sound out words, the other kids laughed at her" (Polacco, 6).

Her heroic teacher, Mr. Falker, discovers her "secret" when he finds her hiding under a stairwell at school. A fellow classmate had bullied her, mocking and poking fun of her on her way to recess. To avoid additional ridicule, Trisha had skipped recess and hidden under the stairwell. Mr. Falker gives her an opportunity to explain why she is hiding. After hearing her stories of shame and humiliation, Mr. Falker begins using multisensory techniques during class and after school to bring the dormant words to life for this struggling reader. Trisha became an avid reader and later, as an adult, a writer.

Another student, "Steven" (now an adult) reported that when he was reading a word at the beginning of a sentence, such as *was*, the same word would appear again near the end of the same sentence, but it would appear differently, becoming, for example, *saw*. As an otherwise bright elementary student, the reading challenge frustrated both Steven and his parents. It seems he was not remembering the same word he had read correctly a few seconds earlier. It also took Steven hours to complete a fifteen-minute homework assignment. It took him just as long to complete, the "do first" board work in school.

Steven was a genius when it came to mechanical manipulations. Around age six and on special occasions, Steven received cars and trucks as gifts from family and friends, which he dismantled just to put them back together. His mother recalled his taking apart complex toy vehicles and meticulously reassembling them.

After struggling through middle and high school, Steven received a high-school certificate—not a high-school diploma. The certificate indicated that he had attended school for twelve years but had not completed standard high-school units required for a high-school diploma. After graduation, Steven got his first job as a custodian in a public school. Unfortunately, one day, he mixed some cleaning liquids, which caused a dangerous toxic chemical fume. Steven was fired. Regretfully, not knowing how to read can indeed be a health risk.

During his years of schooling, Steven's reading disability prevented him from reading at grade level, and no one sought to utilize the strengths of his learning style. Steven's mother conceded that if she and his teachers had understood how to maximize his tactile, "hands-on" learning style early on, life would have been easier for him. He would not have had as many stressful years of doing homework with sweaty palms and headaches. He probably would not have been fired from his first job. And, finally, as a young adult, he would not have had to settle for a minimum-wage job in a fast-food restaurant. With proper interventions, Steven probably could have been listed among those who succeeded despite their learning style or learning differences, such as Albert Einstein, Charles Swab, and James Earl Jones. Steven could have been among outstanding creative geniuses such as writer Hans Christian Andersen; artist, painter, and inventor Leonardo da Vinci; inventor Alexander Graham Bell; and actors Henry Winkler, Whoopi Goldberg, and Tom Cruise.

The literacy report of almost ten years ago remains the same regarding literacy. The US Department of Education maintains that illiteracy is the number-one educational problem in America (NICHD 2001, 2002; President Obama's Address to the Nation 2010). What can educators do? Let's consider some scientific perspectives on what takes place in the reading process, with attention to the functioning of the brain. These perspectives have implications for understanding dyslexia as a learning difference.

Recent studies published by Carnegie Melon University in *Science Daily* (2008) indicate that *remedial instruction* can use the plasticity of the human brain to gain an educational improvement. The findings showed that many areas in the brains of poor readers were activated at near-normal levels immediately after remediation, with only a few areas less active. In addition, when their brains were scanned one year later, the activation differences between good and poor readers had nearly vanished. These findings suggested that the neural gains were strengthened over time, probably due to effective engagement in reading activities. These researchers explained that poor readers initially have less activation in the parietal lobes (top and back portions) and the frontal lobes where decoding the sounds into words, phrases, and sentences are assimilated. However, after the poor readers received remedial treatment, their brains were functioning almost normal or equal to those of good readers (Ibid 2008).

Regardless of this encouraging brain research, school districts attempt to provide universal screening (prescreening) of all students prior to labeling them as poor readers. Some school districts have adopted the three-tier process to ensure that all students have a fair chance at succeeding. Tier 1 provides quality classroom instruction based on a standard curriculum framework; Tier 2 utilizes supplemental instruction that focuses on conceptual gaps assessed in Tier 1; and Tier 3 involves the use of intensive interventions (usually thirty minutes to one hour daily) specifically designed to meet the individual needs of students who did not succeed in Tiers 1 and 2. The term *intensive interventions* is sometimes used interchangeably with *remedial instruction*, which requires direct systematic instruction for one to three students at a time. Progress should be assessed systematically.

Progress monitoring is an ongoing process of assessing student performance, which is measured through informal classroom assessment, benchmark assessment instruments, and/or large-scale assessments (e.g., district or state tests). Progress monitoring should involve three vitally important steps in the intervention plan: (1) identify students as soon as they begin to fall behind; (2) determine if students are making adequate progress within a four- to six-week period; and (3) modify instruction early enough to ensure each student gains essential skills expected for grade-level performance. Remedial instruction facilitated through tiered processes and progress monitoring can aid in activating brain processes that can enhance the performance of students with dyslexic learning differences (State Board Policy: Intervention n.d.).

Brain-Compatible Learning Environments

There are approximately fourteen key principles of brain-compatible learning. Some of the principles listed in this section were shared by a principal during a wonderful district conference on brain research. However, Erlauer (2003) provided additional insight on the subject and it has been adapted here for general information and careful consideration when setting up a classroom or when studying the learning style of a student. For each principle listed in italics, we have added comments and implications associated with the learning process.

Exhibit 1.1: Key Principles of the Brain and the Learning Process

Key Principles	Learning Processes
1. *Uniqueness.* Every brain is totally unique.	Each person has a unique brain just as each has different fingerprints. The brain that has a unique pattern, or wiring, may respond to the environment in different ways.
2. *Impact of threat or high stress.* These alter and impair learning and even kill brain cells.	Stress impacts the way we learn. The brain functions ineffectively under stress.
3. *Emotions are critical to learning.* Emotions drive our attention, meaning and memory.	Anything that is important should be connected to an emotion in order to become a part of memory. People don't pay attention to boring things.
4. *Memory and retrieval pathways are created by sensory stimulation.* Information and experiences are stored in a variety of pathways.	Repetition is important to short and long-term memory. Repeating an idea or sensory activity that helps develop dendrites in the brain is crucial for long-term memory.
5. *All learning is a mind-body function.* Movement, natural foods..., prescribed drugs and chemicals have powerful modulating effects on learning.	Kinesthetic learners learn best when the body is physically engaged. Exercise has been proven to enhance brain power. It is the number one stimulant (*Erlauer*, 2003, p. 52.).
6. *Complex and adaptive system.* Effective change involves an entire complex system. Every brain adapts to its environment based on experience.	In teaching, establishing prior knowledge is crucial with all students, but the student with the dyslexic brain will find it most difficult to create meaning without connecting to past experiences.
7. *Patterns and programs drive understanding.* Intelligence is the ability to elicit and to construct useful patterns.	Graphic organizers empower students in organizing and developing long-term memory by creating a pictured pattern of the content.
8. *The brain is meaning driven.* Meaning is more important to the brain than information.	Meaning can be developed through positive relationships and exposure to a wide variety of people, places, things and ideas.
9. *Rich, non-conscious learning takes place continuously.* We process both parts and wholes simultaneously. We are affected by a great deal of peripheral influences.	A child's brain can be influenced while sleeping. Many parents tell stories or pray over their little ones. Others may sing while the child drifts into a rich, peaceful sleep. These are all brain-developing gestures from the child's first teacher.
10. *The social brain is born at birth.* The brain develops better while interacting with others during early childhood. Social intelligence is fostered in the contextual environments of society.	Humans are social beings. The first emotion a baby learns is love, and without it the brain will not develop physically! (Caine, et al.,2009, p. 9. The child must have sensory stimulation to grow properly as a social being.
11. *Developmental stages are evident during maturation.* Some experiences are better done earlier than later.	Learning to read is an example of an experience if done earlier will be better than later. The child's brain can adapt and learn much faster even if the approach has to be different for most children.
12. *The nature of enrichment should be diverse.* The brain can grow new connections at any age. Complex, challenging and natural interactive experiences with feedback are best. Cognitive skills develop better with music and motor skills.	Utilizing *multiple intelligences* (Armstrong, 2003, pp. 40-45; Gardner, 1999) is the best way to engage the broad cognitive make-up of the brain. The brain can be stimulated at any age if the interest matches the activity.
13. The brain needs high-protein food (e.g., fish and lean meats), stimulation through physical exercises, and sleep for restoration and mental clarity in order to function at its best.	Parents and teachers should provide and encourage children to eat vegetables (raw and cooked), fish and lean meats daily to maintain good health. Physical exercise with plenty of water twenty to thirty minutes at least four times a week will help nurture and aerate the brain.
14. *Self-Organizing and mental organization help the brain remember.* All learning generates new patterns of learning. New behaviors are often unpredictable. The whole system is greater than the sum of the parts.	In other words, learning like a pebble in a pond, has a ripple effect. One pebble of learning encircles more learning and connections.

Source: Brain-based Learning Design Principles, DesignShare n.d.

The overall goal of all reading enhancement programs should be to create ways to empower all kinds of learners to become more successful. Likewise, personnel throughout the school environment should be acclimated to the reading enhancement programs so that necessary support is provided for the students and teachers. By providing effective remedial and intervention services, school administrators would earn more respect for the school as a whole and for the teachers who are committed to making a difference in the lives of the students and families they serve.

Most educators understand that Tier 3 instruction is intensive. In this tier, students should have additional accommodations and adjustments for concepts taught. In other words, accommodations and modifications should be made in the learning environment by providing a range of activities and materials from which learners can choose, while limiting distractions. Proposed tasks should be presented in smaller steps for targeted students but should accomplish the same overall goal for the class. For example, the teacher should extend the length of time to complete the task but allow time frames for segments to be completed leading up to the final date. During this time, opportunities for student responses and feedback should be provided.

Sometimes, the problem-based learning activities will cause these young creative thinkers to offer better student-friendly ways of presenting the assigned project. For example, in an urban middle-school class that had a larger "street" vocabulary than standard English, we capitalized on the students' verbal strengths and invited their input. The class was assigned a massive project of creating a *Dictionary from the Hood*. One group was responsible for interviewing people in the school's community (young and old) to find words used currently as well as slang words from previous generations. Students had to follow the format of the dictionary, providing the origin and indicating if the word was obsolete. The second team had to sort the words into parts of speech, with examples of each. The third team's responsibility was to record the definitions of the words with first and second meanings. The fourth team combined the parts for each word and recorded the synthesized definition in the *Dictionary from the Hood*. Because the information was novel and fresh, students literally rushed into English class with great anticipation to work on their respective tasks within the allotted time frame of the first fifteen to twenty minutes of class. The class average test scores in language arts improved an average of eight points that school semester. The areas of strength were now dictionary skills, spelling, and vocabulary for this sixth-grade English/language arts class. Noteworthy was that this change was facilitated through employing some of the key principles in the activity. The environment for learning was compatible for enhancing brain functions.

Perspectives of School Administrators

Because school budgets and other resources are often limited, school administrators frequently express concerns that special programs and accommodations are too costly.

In addition, instructional personnel are progressively harder to identify and/or train for the minimum of 5 percent of the students exhibiting reading/language difficulties. The state of the economy at the end of the Bush administration in 2008 also caused school administrators to argue that they hardly had adequate funds to purchase supplementary resources for the majority (80 percent)—not to mention the 5 percent with special needs. However, administrative stakeholders know that the cost of *not* accommodating those who have reading difficulties and who do not qualify for special education will cost more for society in the long run. There is ample research to support this premise (Lyons 2004, 2006). Public school systems, regardless of financial circumstances, are expected to provide quality instruction for all students.

If students, for instance, are illiterate in third grade, they have a one-in-eight chance of catching up and remaining on or near grade level (Beck and Juel 2001). Students who read two or more grade levels below average by the end of middle school usually drop out before graduating from high school. These dropouts add significantly to the approximately ten million who drop out each year.

Lyons (2004), the former lead researcher of the National Institute for Child Health and Human Development (NICHD), classified illiteracy as a health risk. It affects all areas of human existence and sustainability. Additionally, if students are not literate by adulthood, they suffer great personal loss, and the general society loses millions of dollars in unearned wages, taxes, and revenues that support social and educational services. The National Institute for Child Health and Human Development also reported that approximately 70 percent of those incarcerated are struggling readers who often exhibit characteristics of dyslexia. It costs taxpayers over $35,000 to house and care for each prisoner. This is much more than the amount needed to remediate a student's reading difficulty or to give a full scholarship for a student to attend a college or university. It is, therefore, imperative that educators address the needs of different learners early.

Summary of Chapter Points

For the struggling student with the characteristics of dyslexia, reading can be a demanding task to face daily. Classroom reading (language) success is possible for most of these students when academic programming includes accurate assessments of specific reading behaviors and instructional strategies tailored to students' reading characteristics. Major points included in chapter 1 are the following:

- Dyslexia is a composite of multidimensional characteristics.
- There is a broad misconception of dyslexia.
- A large number of dyslexic students are neglected or underserved.
- Understanding key principles of the brain-compatible learning styles may empower learning.

Below are some websites that provide a broad range of activities and interventions that include the five components of reading: phonemic awareness, phonics, fluency, vocabulary development, and comprehension. Information from these sites can be incorporated in activities suggested in "Teaching Tips."

Teaching Tips

1. Engage students in diverse activities to encourage interest; present learning tasks in smaller steps for targeted students and provide longer time periods for completion if needed.
2. Encourage peer sharing but avoid placing a student in a stressful situation.

Suggested Websites

Websites for Reading Skills and Vocabulary Development	
Brain Pop http://www.brainpop.com	Exercises for the body and brain that will help get and maintain attention and provide tips for beginners in their first school.
First School http://www.firstschool.com	Beginning reading skills from phonics to downloadable stories to read at school and at home.
Star Fall http://www.starfall.com	Introductory lessons and games in math that are meaningful to the young "mathematician."
My Fun Brain http://www.myfunbrain.com	Fun things to do to exercise the brain from kindergarten to third grade.
My Quiz Hub http://www.myquizhub.com	Fun ways to take quizzes and create quizzes.
Vocabulary.com http://www.vocabulary.com	Links to vocabulary development
One Look http://www.onelook.com/index.html	Links to several word development programs

Suggested Readings/Resources

Erlauer, L. 2003. *The brain-compatible classroom: Using what we do know about learning to improve teacher.* Alexandria, VA: Association for Supervision and Curriculum Development.

Lackney, J. A. n.d. "12 Design Principles Based on Brain-based Learning Research." DesignShare: The International Forum for Innovative Schools. Retrieved from www.designshare.com/Research/BrainBasedLearn98.htm.

Mississippi Department of Education. 2005. State Board Policy: Intervention Process. Retrieved from www.mde.k12.ms.us/docs/policy-manual/4300.htm?sfvrsn=2.

Polacco, P (1998). Thank you, Mr. Falker. New York, NY: Philomel Books.

CHAPTER 2

Different Reading Styles and Environmental Factors

Chapter Subheadings
The Dyslexic Reading Style and Related Difficulties
The Learning-Different Student
Dyslexia: Nature or Nurture?
Impoverished Environments and Educational Risk Factors

OBJECTIVE
To describe dyslexia as a reading difficulty that may evolve for various reasons and requires teacher intervention strategies.

TERMS TO KNOW
Different reading styles: the diverse ways (visual, auditory, spatial, linguistic) students approach learning to reading.

IDEA guidelines: federal regulations included in the Individuals with Disability Education Act.

504 Plan: an instructional plan for students who do not qualify for IDEA, designed to remove barriers that inhibit the individual's learning and allow accommodations in some major documented areas.

Struggling readers: readers who show greater than average difficulty in decoding words and communicating using common methods of oral and written expression; often referred to as signs of dyslexia.

Dyslexia is a reading style that includes both the learner and the learner's reading process. Because the characteristics are so interwoven, many experts would rather not label these students as dyslexic but refer to them as struggling readers. Additionally, many concerned parents of profoundly dyslexic children would like their child to receive help but would prefer a substitute for the "demeaning" label. However, not all parents and students feel demeaned by the term. Older students, for example, are generally relieved when they discover that their language-reading difficulty has a name and that there are many helpful intervention programs and services that can support them. As presented in chapter 1, and paraphrased here, dyslexia is an inherited reading/language learning disability that is generally evident by an inability to decode words and communicate using common methods of oral and written expression, which includes spelling phonetically.

When students are made aware that they are not alone with a given reading difficulty and that 5 to 20 percent of the population shares similar difficulties, they tend to feel less excluded. Although the reading styles among struggling students may be as different as fingerprints, their learning styles are usually multisensory, meaning they need to encompass three or more of the five senses. The common thread or paramount issue among different learners with similar learning difficulties is that they often do not get adequate help with their reading/language deficiencies before third grade. When the academic needs of students are not addressed in a timely manner, these students try to develop compensatory strategies to master concepts on their own or they learn to "get by" in school. These academic "outsiders," left on the fringes, are often described as slow learners and/or are placed in special-education classes and special learning groups. This situation often results in these students becoming so frustrated with school that they drop out for (what they think is) a more doable and less stressful environment.

In an urban school district of about 31,000 students, an action research study was conducted by M. Crocket to identify potentially at-risk students. From this student population, 994 students were referred to the District Support Team (DST) for review and to determine if further assessment was necessary. Of that number, 550 students were recommended for comprehensive evaluations. Based on the results of the study , it was found that 451 students (or 82 percent) were eligible for exceptional education services. The other students (18 percent) were ineligible for these services. Of this number, 90 percent was male, and 10 percent was female. Since approximately 20 percent is the estimated number of students who would likely have characteristics of dyslexia in any given population, the ineligible 18 percent is statistically on target. Also, 90 percent of the same student population with reading problems scored higher than expected in most subject and skill areas on the Woodcock-Johnson Tests of Cognitive Abilities and, therefore, did not qualify for special education.

The Dyslexic Reading Style and Related Reading Difficulties

One of the most misunderstood reading disabilities is dyslexia. In her highly respected research described in *Overcoming Dyslexia*, Sally Shaywitz refers to dyslexia as the hidden disability. It affects about 80 percent of all other reading disabilities combined (NICHD 2004).

The Orton Dyslexia Society defines dyslexia as a specific language-based disorder that is characterized by difficulties in single-word decoding, writing, or spelling despite quality instruction, intelligence, or economic status. The reader should be cognizant and reminded that dyslexia is a reading disorder that affects millions of people all over the world. In American schools, students with characteristics of dyslexia are often misdiagnosed and considered to be slow learners, daydreamers, rebellious, or of low intelligence. These perceptions are unfounded and need to change. When a teacher working with an older student exhibiting characteristics of dyslexia has a flawed perception of that student, the student is likely to become frustrated, which can lead to aggressive behavior or low self-esteem. As stated previously, students with ADD often exhibit behavioral problems along with reading difficulties.

Identifying the specific origin of the reading disability is one of the most difficult challenges teachers face when instructing students with unique reading styles, especially in the upper grades. For instance, there are students who pronounce words correctly and can read a passage but cannot readily comprehend what they are reading. Others can comprehend when read to or questioned orally but cannot correctly respond in writing. Then, there is the bottom 5 to 20 percent with varying deficiencies that may not be able to decode single-syllable words or use the alphabetic principles to apply the letter-sound patterns that properly form words in writing and spelling. The majority of research findings on students with reading disorders reveals that these conditions occur in about 20 percent of the student population (National Institute for Child Health and Human Development 2004). Likewise, other researchers (Lyon and Chhabra 2004; Shaywitz 2003) have studied the functions of the brain as related to reading ability and substantiated that mild to severe dyslexic tendencies can exist in humans as frequently as one in five.

To assist educators in simplifying the process of identifying students within the general population of struggling readers, an instrument is provided in chapter

4 that will aid in identifying the weaknesses and determining the best strategy to accommodate the students. The "Checklist for Identifying Characteristics of Dyslexia or Related Reading Difficulties" was developed over a five-year period by studying struggling readers and observing and assisting teachers in identifying characteristics of dyslexia in a public school district that served approximately 31,000 students in grades K–12. The instrument is included in this book to assist teachers and administrators in identifying the reading styles of students and hopefully in designing the proper strategies, interventions, and accommodations for students with reading disorders such as dyslexia. Counselors or persons recommending the instructional strategies for teachers should have some prior professional training and experience in working with students with reading disorders. In addition, teachers and other professionals involved should be able to determine if and when external professional assistance is needed.

The 504 Plan

The 504 Plan is designed for students who do not meet the eligibility requirements of the Individuals with Disability Education Act (IDEA) but may need accommodations within the general education curriculum. Through the plan, a student is provided access to an education equal to his or her peers, with the disclaimer of "no guarantee for success." Each school district should ensure the following functions of the local 504 team (some schools call it the teacher-support team):

1. Remove barriers that inhibit the individual's learning.
2. Allow accommodations in some major documented areas (e.g., test-taking methods [oral or written], test scores, interventions, doctors/medical reports, attendance records, behavior, and cumulative records).

The individual must have a disability that creates a substantial limitation in a life area of learning or behavior. Based on medical reports, for example, one may notice that there is a health problem that was caused by a birth defect or accident during childhood. Reviewing such documents will help members of the teacher-support team to work together in finding solutions to the learning deficiency. This is probably why some educators refer to IDEA as the Integrated Disability Education Awareness program.

When it is determined that a student has a learning limitation, teachers may accommodate the student by allowing him or her extended time during test taking; having the student take tests in a quiet or isolated environment (when distractions are deterrents for success); and giving the student assignments in smaller segments yet on the same grade level as his or her peers. In other words, accommodate the student by making adjustments to the assignment without changing the concept or level of complexity. *Modifying* is sometimes confused with accommodation. Modifying would be to change the level of work to make it easier. The latter is what teachers are allowed to do in special education, even though most states regardless of a student's educational status require that all students are tested with the same state test.

When working with older students (fourth grade and above) or those with profound reading differences, it may be necessary to seek long-term accommodations. If the parent requests a 504 Plan, usually a certified dyslexia therapist, a certified dyslexia testing specialist, or an expert in reading disabilities should screen or test the student and provide a written analysis with an interpretation of the scores. Some states, such as Texas and Mississippi, require school districts to screen for characteristics of dyslexia and provide the appropriate accommodations for the identified students (Mississippi Department of Education 2009, 69). If the student is not eligible for special education according to the current IDEA guidelines but shows some signs of disability that would impede long-term success, parents can request special accommodations through a 504 Plan. Most states do not require school districts to test for dyslexia, but all state departments and some school districts have local teams, as mentioned earlier, who can guide parents through the process when it is requested. Regardless of state requirements, it is crucial that a process is established for students in the early grades to diagnose possible reading disorders. Be reminded also that the characteristics of dyslexia in most student populations range from mild to profound. The final screening results or diagnosis should be carefully assessed and accommodated so that learning can begin immediately.

Usually, a qualified examiner will use six or more different tests to probe the major areas of the brain that affect the way a child perceives, reproduces, and interprets print. Two comprehensive screening tests that have been used effectively in evaluating the different areas of the brain that may impact one's ability to read are the Pre-Reading Screening Procedures (1997) to identify first-grade academic needs, and the Slingerland Screening Tests for Identifying Children with Specific Language Disability. More specifically, Slingerland tests can assess the following weak areas of struggling readers: memory, auditory processing, phonics, reading word lists, reading fluency, copying from the board, writing in response to reading, and spelling. There are also other diagnostic instruments that can be used to test specific areas of the brain such as the Test of Word Reading Efficiency (TOWRE) and the Test of Written Spelling, Fourth Edition (TWS-4). If the goal of assessment is to accommodate and improve achievement of the learner, then screening instruments such as the Slingerland have been sufficient for this purpose. The general goal of assessment should be to identify the strengths and weaknesses that exist. The screening results would then allow examiners and teachers to know where to start and how to differentiate instruction.

The *Checklist for Reading Styles and Related Behavioral Differences* (see page 51) may be used to determine the learning style of students displaying reading disorders. This procedure should be followed by a more comprehensive screening instrument or test to determine if special therapeutic accommodations are needed. After completing the *Checklist for Reading Styles and Related Behavioral Differences*, the examiner or teacher can refer to chapter two, which presents strategies for the respective learning styles. Recommendations and a list of resources are also provided to support and address the diverse needs of children with learning differences.

The Learning-Different Student

Most observant educators are cognizant of the characteristics of students who are on the "fringes of society" in terms of their reading abilities and general achievement. In addition, educators are usually familiar with some instructional strategies that could be used in assisting these students in moving toward the mainstream of the classroom and society. To formulate these instructional strategies, parents, teachers, and administrators should collaborate on common goals that include both student achievement and student behavior. The parent, the child's first teacher, should be able to identify basic learning differences in the child at an early age if there are any. Secondly, the first schoolteacher should be able to continue the instructional strategies initiated by the parent so that learning for the child is seamless. Therefore, it is crucial that parents are actively involved in the educational process both at home and school. It is important that teachers collaborate horizontally (across subject areas in the same grade) and vertically (among different grade levels) so that the learning process is seamless and continuous. Without proper early interventions and systematic instruction, students who begin school behind their peers in reading readiness skills will often fall further behind their peers as they go up the educational ladder. According to the Consortium of Reading Excellence (2004), these students usually become the struggling readers who have a one-in-eight chance of catching up. It is much better for the students and less costly to the school, district, and state to focus on learning difficulties in the early grades. Intervening in later years costs approximately three dollars for every dollar that would have been spent earlier.

In addition to the crucial time table of the brain, the National Institute of Child Health and Human Development (NICHD) warns us of misplaced talent that is too often deferred. If 5 to 20 percent of students have mild to profound characteristics of dyslexia, they could also have average to above-average intelligence. Many students with reading disabilities have been placed in gifted classes and advanced academic programs because the examiner was screening for levels of intelligence, not reading skills. Learning-different students many times have strengths in creativity, the fine arts, critical thinking, and/or problem solving. Research has found that about 5 percent of students with average to above-average intelligence may also come from low socioeconomic environments where students were seldom read to and/or experienced tragedy early in life. Consequently, this group may display behavioral problems that distract from developing necessary academic skills but have the potential to succeed. Some home-school connections that involve and train parents have been successful in modifying family routines to enhance student performance.

Most teachers know of students who become successful even though they are from families with inherited disabilities or environmental limitations. Therefore, it is important to encourage parents to be supportive and avoid, for example, comparing abilities among family members. A child's innate potential and motivation could defy either or both of these circumstances and succeed. An example that comes to mind is Stacie. She is a high-school student whose mother was single, unemployed, and had a drug habit. The family of four—mother, two girls, and a boy—ended up homeless, and the mother was away from her children most of the time. Stacie, the oldest, became the caregiver for herself and two younger siblings as long as she could, collecting uneaten fruit from classmates at school and hiding whatever she could in her coat pockets. A teacher learned about the situation and reported the family to the school counselor and social worker. With housing, support services, and resources, Stacie and her siblings almost immediately became honor students in their respective schools. Years later, she graduated from high school with honors and scored high on the American College Test. Stacie received offers from various colleges and universities and accepted one that offered a full scholarship with other necessary support. Stacie later became a successful medical doctor. This story is told here just to support the point that some children can succeed even if they do not have basic needs, as long as they have potential and motivation. Then there are others who may have nurturing parents and all their basic needs met, but who still do not succeed. Usually, if one is born in a family of affluence and inherits a learning difference, it could be a disorder called dyslexia. The reinforcing point here is that in both environments, strategic accommodations are necessary for the struggling student to succeed.

There is a difference between dyslexia (an inherited neurological brain structure that causes difficulty in processing language) and a struggling reader who may have the mental and physiological abilities but has not been taught. The latter is what one astute educator called "dys-taughtia." Attention in this chapter is given to identifying dyslexia and its origin along with similar disorders. Focus is directed to common characteristics and some recommendations for supporting students who are challenged with these learning characteristics.

Dyslexia: Nature or Nurture?

Dyslexia is considered to be of neurological and genetic origin. This condition is known to appear more profoundly in someone who has a parent or other close relative with a similar condition. General reading difficulties that cannot be alleviated with quality instruction are different from difficulties, such as dyslexia, that require therapeutic strategies to remediate. Some reading difficulties can be *acquired dyslexia*, caused by an injury to the head or similar external factors. However, it is important to know that dyslexic characteristics can be described as unique functions of the brain. It is imperative to understand that these methodic brain functions, when students engage in the reading process, may be different from those of struggling readers who are from impoverished environments. For example, struggling readers from impoverished backgrounds may have poor reading readiness skills and limited vocabulary because reading was not seen as a priority in the home and/or they were seldom read to. These children may or may not be dyslexic. If they are found to also be dyslexic, the reading difficulties are compounded.

Generally, the left hemisphere of the cerebrum is the controlling unit of the brain when it comes to reading, writing, spelling, decoding, and manipulating letters and sounds of the English language and symbols in mathematics. The cerebrum, the largest part of the human brain, consists of a right hemisphere and a left hemisphere. The dyslexic person tends to have neurological sensors (wiring) in the left hemisphere of the brain that do not interpret what is seen and heard in the same way that most others do. Scientists report that the right hemisphere is dominant and slightly larger in most instances in people with dyslexia. The right hemisphere of the brain is wired to deal with talents and skills associated with creativity, such as the fine arts, drama, sports, philosophy, and out-of-the-box problem solving. Many dyslexics with a dominant right hemisphere are creative and talented. However, an individual with dyslexia could also have two hemispheres of equal size or a weak corpus callosum. Any of these conditions in the brain can contribute to dyslexia.

The corpus callosum is a large bundle of fibers situated like a bridge between the left and right cerebral hemispheres. These 300 million fibers relay information from regions in one lobe to regions in the other four lobes (frontal, temporal, parietal, and occipital). Each lobe serves a different role and the corpus callosum is the major conductor in organizing auditory stimuli and in language perception. The corpus callosum sends information to the proper side of the brain for processing. However, in some dyslexics, information that should travel to the right hemisphere is sent to the left hemisphere or vice versa. This often causes mental chaos. For example, if the corpus callosum does not transmit information that is seen, heard, or felt into the proper areas in the brain, the person experiences frustration. Studies have shown that interruptions in areas located in the cerebrum can also contribute to common characteristics of dyslexia as evident in language acquisition and written communication.

The cerebrum contributes to the processing and communication of information. In this regard, dyslexics can usually communicate effectively in other ways that don't require manipulating symbols of language, such as art, music, acting, singing, mathematics, and science. Teachers who are the most successful in accommodating the learning styles of dyslexic students discover their strengths and build the needed brain-friendly language skills through those areas of strength.

Impoverished environments can inhibit the mental development of young children to the extent that they may mimic the characteristics of dyslexia. Even though this may be the case, this section will elaborate on dyslexia as an inherited condition. It is important that the reader understands that the dyslexic's brain is wired differently. As explained previously, this condition is one of several learning disabilities characterized by difficulties in reading, writing, spelling, comprehension, listening, speaking, and memory. The dyslexic student who has one of these characteristics may be screened as an individual with mild dyslexic characteristics, while other individuals could have two or more of the above-mentioned characteristics and be classified as having moderate to severe characteristics of dyslexia. When a child has most of these characteristics, it is highly recommended that the child is properly identified so that a certified therapist can prepare an analysis for teachers and or school administrators to follow up with parents or guardians in providing needed interventions and accommodations.

The Learning Disabilities Association of America (2003) explains that many children, including children with learning disabilities, do not learn to read in the first grade because they lack the basic readiness skills or the school's method is not appropriate for them. Too many school districts still allow students to repeat grades two or three times without effective interventions. Unless these children are identified early and appropriate interventions are provided, they may be passed from one grade level to the next (called social promotion) prior to receiving proper remediation services. Repeating grades multiple times often happens when appropriate reading instruction is not available in the regular classroom after the reading problems are initially identified. Concerning this, Reid Lyons asserts that quality reading programs must be available across grade levels if we are to significantly reduce illiteracy. After interventions and accommodations have been made, students will continue to need direct reading instruction, which may be one-on-one or small-group instruction (Lyons 2001).

In an action research study conducted in an urban school district in the state of Mississippi, it was discovered that many educators did not understand the scope and diversity of language disabilities that exist in a typical classroom. However, as these educators were trained through professional development workshops and onsite modeling, it was found that the knowledge base and performance level of teachers working with reading disabilities were enhanced, and so was the level of student achievement. This was evident in the results of a small grant program where about $26,000 was awarded to serve the students who had characteristics of dyslexia in this particular school district. Descriptions were given about the targeted students before the intervention was administered, and afterward, noted improvements of the students were recorded for a period of six months for the targeted students. One student had enrolled just three months before the school year ended. Due to a strong possibility of retention, a first-grade student joined the class in March of the same school year in hopes that the intense systematic interventions would help him make the grade. Scores from DIBELS were not substantial, but they indicated a form of growth for 80 percent of the students enrolled. Two or more skills were assessed, but only the test of Oral Reading Fluency (ORF) was recorded to show how one may chart progress monitoring. Ideally, there should have been a pretest, midyear test, and a year-end test. Exhibit 2.1 contains 2007–2008 dyslexia data for the end-of-year report on elementary-level participants.

Exhibit 2.1: Greenleaf School

Teachers	Student	Grade	DIBELS*** or SF** Pre-Test (Baseline)	DIBELS*** or SF** Spring (Post-test)	District 1st Term	District 3rd Term	Fall Report card grades in LA/Reading	Spring Report card Grades in LA/Reading
1. Collins	BR	3rd			68 Reading 72 Language	72 Reading 92 Language	72/68	80/80
2. Elliot	ZL	2nd	ORF* 18	ORF* 11			52/68	74/72
3. Elliott	DR	2nd	ORF* 35	ORF* 23			68/60	86/77
4. Collins	JB	3rd	ORF* 23	ORF* 25			80/92	77/80
5. Collins	JT	3rd	ORF* 46	ORF* 48			80/88	82/83

*ORF= Oral Reading Fluency
**SF= Scott Foresman Tests
***DIBELS (Elementary Developmental Assessment Instrument)

The similarities among fundamental reading skills of dyslexic elementary students and those of high-school students were amazing. At one high school, two eleventh-grade students had difficulties that needed strategic systematic interventions in phonics and fluency. Based on the amount of growth observed, each student improved about two grade levels in a period of six months. Remember, this was high school, and according to research-based programs, these students would need to know the rules to apply when faced with unfamiliar words. Two students were familiar with the alphabet but could not recall the sequence of the letters and their corresponding sounds. To get by, these students memorized the shapes of words or the beginning letter sound of each word. Now in high school, too often they guessed incorrectly and paused for help when multisyllable words appeared in the reading assignment. Thus, the teacher followed all steps of the chosen intervention program but did not feel the need to spend as much time reviewing initial letter recognition, for example, beyond the guidance given by the linguist in the Texas Scottish Rite Dyslexia Training Program, provided on an instructional DVD. The need to move slower or faster was determined by the facilitator on a student-by-student basis.

Having an effective intervention resource helped teachers in the trial program to become more confident in working with students with reading disabilities. The procedures and strategies utilized were more consistently implemented when it was discovered that this multisensory method was the most effective way to reach severely struggling readers. Other teachers who were not using the Texas Scottish Rite Dyslexia Training Program began using similar intervention programs such as Language! and READ 180 to meet the diverse reading styles. However, this district did not see measureable difference in test scores until district-wide training was provided for teachers and school administrators. Trainers from Consortium of Reading Excellence (CORE) were contracted to train instructional specialists, literacy specialists, and about twenty-seven lead teachers. They were strategically selected from the respective eight school feeder patterns of this urban school district. The charge was to master the multiple dimensions of teaching reading along with intervention strategies and appropriate assessments for all students in K–12. Teachers from kindergarten through high school filled the reading training sessions to capacity. After participating in professional development trainings, more of the teachers and certified tutors in the district reported a higher level of confidence when working with struggling readers across grade and ability levels. Over a period of four years and fueled by the No Child Left Behind mandate, teachers in the district implemented appropriate teaching strategies and accommodations for approximately 31,000 students. In 2006, the district's student achievement level ranked among the highest in the state with more than 95 percent of the fifty-eight schools being ranked as "successful" or "advanced." No *teacher* was left behind. Therefore, very few children were left behind.

Implementing a common strategy to train all teachers and support staff and teachers was a monumental task for the district's superintendent and district instructional training specialists. Requiring school leaders, teachers, and key administrators to become familiar with the basic techniques of reading equipped them to teach or influence all kinds of teachers for diverse learners on all levels and from various environmental circumstances throughout the district. There were still educational challenges to face.

As experts in human development can attest, impoverished environments can inhibit the proper formation of the brain during prenatal development of the unborn child. Early intervention is imperative, providing good nutrition and an emotionally healthy environment for the mother-to-be. After the child is born, learning begins. Students reared in severely impoverished environments frequently develop learning impediments that mimic the characteristics of dyslexia and sometimes ADD. Proper training of teachers and key school leaders is crucial for identifying learning differences and making referrals.

However, there are some distinct differences between hereditary or acquired brain disorders and those that have functional deficits due to impoverished environments (Slingerland 2001. Though both will likely require multisensory stimulation to modify the brain, a student with a reading disability will require therapeutic, prescriptive instruction. A student who has no disability but lacks exposure to a nurturing environment may have similar scores in the beginning, but with educational interventions and systematic instruction, this student may perform better and improve at a faster rate than the student with a diagnosed disability, even though the latter does not come from an impoverished home. The circumstances surrounding poverty can affect a student's vocabulary and general exposure to the world, but the student's innate ability will allow him or her to catch up if circumstances change.

Real-life accounts show differences in students with hereditary or acquired brain disorders and those with functional deficits related to impoverished environments. Tyrone's parents were young evangelists and moved two or three times when he was four and would have been attending kindergarten. They did not enroll Tyrone in kindergarten because they thought it would be too stressful for him, trying to keep up with the other students while changing schools several times, so they kept him at home. He was the youngest of three in the family. During the day, he ran errands with his parents and had educational conversations about whatever they were doing together but received no formal instruction. At five and a half, he finally entered kindergarten. He did not know the entire alphabet nor did he understand how to associate letters and sounds to form words. Within six weeks, Tyrone had memorized the letters and understood how to match sounds, even some irregular sounds, to form words. Tyrone was not a struggling reader with characteristics of dyslexia. He was one of the fortunate 5 percent that needed little guidance in learning to read, regardless of his irregular environmental circumstances.

Sean is an example of another kind of learner who was born into a nurturing educational environment but still had reading difficulties. Typically, Sean struggled like a child born in poverty but in a different way. The deficiency in decoding and language development skills required immediate direct, systematic, multisensory instruction. In addition, Sean did not get the support he needed during kindergarten and the early grades. Consequently, he was placed in special-education classes in third grade. Teacher training is very important in situations like these. When teachers know the characteristics of dyslexia, they can better accommodate the learning difference and are more focused on addressing the reading difficulty and less concerned about labeling students.

Administrators and most educators are reluctant about labeling students dyslexic for good reasons. Most educators do not want to misdiagnose a learning difference that could be a related disorder. However, we have found that dyslexic students, and most parents who have experienced similar problems in school, are relieved to discover the reading disorder has a name. When parents detect a learning difference in their child and have the child officially tested, inside or outside the school district, the diagnosis should be accepted by the district and appropriate accommodations should be provided as soon as possible. Students with unique learning styles, like dyslexia, should not be left behind. It is the law practiced in some states (Mississippi Department of Education, Special Education Division—IDEA 1997).

How can educators help struggling readers who are often left behind? All too often, the answer to this question is oversimplified. Teachers, with a relatively few exceptions, want to promote student learning and enhance student achievement. Teachers are the single most important resource in the classroom. Therefore, they should be well educated and knowledgeable about student learning styles and the craft of teaching. To effectively help struggling readers, teachers need to understand diverse cultures that may be presented in their classroom from year to year. Marzano (2011a) emphasizes the importance of developing positive and supportive relationships with students. The bonding between teachers and students occurs more from what the teacher *does* with students than from sympathetic attitudes generated by *what is known* about students. This issue is particularly crucial with students who are already challenged by self-esteem issues coupled with learning difficulties.

In large classes, personal attention may be difficult to arrange with students, especially at the beginning of the school year. Effective teachers often assign a one- or two-page autobiography that includes interests, hobbies, favorite things, favorite classes, and career goals. After reviewing these autobiographies, the teacher can then classify them according to interests, hobbies, or the like so that establishing small, compatible groups within the classroom can be easily and more effectively organized. This strategy allows teachers to capitalize, early, on the strengths and interests of students in the class. Students also tend to respond more positively when teachers call them by name. The traditional seating charts are still effective at the beginning of school for matching names and faces in assigned spaces.

To assist in the bonding process, teachers can also generate one-on-one conversations about areas of interests as well as select a few areas of general interest in small groups. Subjects such as sports and favorite TV shows can also initiate discussions and provide opportunities for students to separate opinions from facts, which can then be written about or debated.

Teachers can accommodate challenged learners in a variety of ways. For example, if a student does not readily understand a classroom assignment, and is lagging behind, another student who finishes early, can assist that student. Teachers should have various resources available in the classroom, so that the concepts taught, can be presented from tangible to abstract (less advanced to advanced) allowing more opportunities for mastery among diverse students. Generally, teachers should promote a caring environment for diverse learners even when it is tempting to verbally retaliate when a student "acts out." Ideally, a student should never be openly embarrassed or shamed regardless of the age, grade level, or learning circumstance.

Understanding unique individual learning styles is important regardless of class size even though it may be a challenge for the teacher. Though students with learning differences make up a relatively small percentage of the classroom, they can become restless and disrupt the whole class if not carefully accommodated with appropriate interventions. As one frustrated veteran teacher put it, "If we identify a student as dyslexic, we should be prepared to teach him/her. We need time set aside for this or provided assistance. Currently, we are instructed to complete paperwork and document, document, and document!" This teacher later received the requested assistance because she was one of those trained in the district mentioned earlier. It is important that school administrators, instructional specialists, literacy coaches, and paraprofessionals, such as certified tutors, respond to the needs of teachers wherever possible and as soon as possible. Other support and alternative strategies are available free online, or nearly free, for teachers to support different learners.

The Resource Section of this book lists many resources and creative ways to reach the different or reticent learner. In addition to having students write about personal experiences, teachers can bring in community speakers or parents with unique hobbies, interests, and careers to share with the students. After each class session, students can then discuss and collectively compile a list of what interested them the most. Teachers should help students use graphic organizers to align their thoughts before writing. Then, follow up with a paragraph about personal and vicarious experiences. These kinds of activities can broaden students' background knowledge as well as cultivate student-to-student and students-to-teacher relationships within the instructional process.

The authors have observed both ineffective and effective instructional strategies being used during the process of teaching. One example of an ineffective assignment occurred in an urban school where the common practice was to isolate struggling readers and/or disruptive students from the main group. This day it was a struggling nonreader who was excluded during the reading block. The student was in a corner completing a workbook page that required him to color a picture when finished. After class, the teacher and instructional specialist reflected on the reading lesson, being careful to respect the teacher's efforts. When asked about the individualized student assignment, she responded, "That student is just so far behind in his reading! He hardly reads at all! It would take too much of my time to help him catch up." Unfortunately, as many studies support, the majority of this underserved student population of diverse learners are male. They are usually found sitting behind room dividers, isolated in corners of classrooms, or sitting close to the teacher's desk.

Introductory Steps toward Differentiating Instruction

There are several steps teachers can take to effectively address the learning differences of struggling readers. The following steps have worked successfully for many teachers:

1. Pretest the student or review existing test data on the student's existing strengths and weaknesses in key subject areas.
2. Seek suggestions from the grade-level teacher-support team.
3. Discuss the team's assessments and recommendations with the school counselor and/or principal for specific needs.
4. Check online for free or almost-free resources for teachers (see websites at the end of this chapter).
5. Customize instruction for different learners enabling them to
    a. have a common understanding of content;
    b. learn how to process new information;
    c. assimilate it with what they already know;
    d. organize it in the brain; and
    e. share it with others. (See relevant websites at the end of this chapter.)

Impoverished Environments and Educational Risk Factors

During the last decade, various studies have indicated that the top five family risk factors that affect the reading level of children are the following:

1. The mother has less than a high-school education.
2. The mother speaks a language other than English as her primary language.
3. The mother was unmarried at the time of the child's birth.

4. The family lives below the official poverty line (based on Food Service guidelines from the US Department of Agriculture for free or reduced meals).
5. Only one parent or guardian is present in the home on a regular basis.

Of these five risk factors, the studies revealed that the number-one indicator of a student being at risk was the mother having less than a high-school education and placing little value on the educational process or its merit. These top five indicators of at-risk characteristics may affect student performance but may *not* be a physical or measurable disability. In a report by the National Center for Education Statistics, it was revealed that one-half of today's preschoolers are affected by at least one of these risk factors and 15 percent are affected by three or more of them. Children with one or more of these characteristics may be educationally disadvantaged or at risk of school failure.

The Kaiser State Health Facts of Mississippi reported in 2009 that, in a state population of 2,889,110, 27.4 percent were at the poverty level, compared to the United States poverty rate of 17.2 percent. The report also showed 43.6 percent of African Americans were at or below the poverty level in Mississippi while the percentage of Caucasians was 16.1 percent. The national poverty rate for African Americans is 32.2 percent compared to 11.5 percent for Caucasians. It's important to note that students from low-income families are 2.4 times more likely to drop out of school than students from middle- or upper-income families, regardless of race.

Bob Wise, president of the Alliance for Excellent Education (*Washington Journal, C-Span Television Show*, October, 2009) also provides some alarming statistics on consequences of poor education of America's youth: 7,000 drop out daily, 1.2 million drop out each year. Only 33 percent of students now in ninth grade will be ready for college after high-school graduation. Poorly prepared students in a globally competitive workforce cause an estimated $35 billion loss per year in wages. These poorly prepared students are the ones we are trying to reach. They want to be helped probably more than we want to help them, but to save their image among their peers, many opt to empower themselves by appearing preoccupied and apathetic. These are the hard-to-reach-and-teach students who challenge even well-prepared and dedicated teachers.

Most authentic sources also indicate that, under normal circumstances, boys tend to catch up with girls in language arts by third grade. On tests, males may even surpass girls in math and science at this age. School leaders who are from a different culture from their students may find it difficult to address the social and academic needs of a large population of at-risk students. Consequently, students should be taught with hands-on, multisensory interventions that promote learning in ways these students learn best.

If not, this targeted group will likely fail as students and become less-than-successful adults. Without a direct, systematic, multisensory teaching approach, the outcome for struggling students is usually poor grades. Additionally, at-risk students generally have poor attendance records due to severe illnesses such as asthmatic conditions that are neglected or improperly treated, tragic experiences coupled with unsafe conditions in the home, frequent relocation of family in different school zones, unacceptable behavior (including suspensions), and/or few role models among the significant others in their home and community. These students generally acquire low self-esteem and rebel in the classroom, jeopardizing the education of others, as well as their own, in the educational environment.

Before they drop out, many of these students have repeated two or more grades and have been identified as overage for their current grade. Sometimes the school administrator takes the approach of placing the at-risk student in the proper grade with peers by skipping a grade or two to make the age more compatible with the numerical grade. This approach leaves the student more frustrated than before. Many students give up and drop out by ninth grade or by age sixteen, whichever comes first. They often console themselves and explain to school officials and parents that they will seek a general education degree (GED) and get a job. But many lack academic prerequisites for most subjects and lack sufficient discipline to complete these tasks on their own.

The next chapter addresses undisciplined behavior that could be a side effect of inappropriate instruction and unfair assessments. Many times the behavior—hereditary or learned—result in added frustrations for the struggling reader and for those who share his or her learning environment.

Summary of Chapter Points
Major points included in this chapter are the following:

- Flawed perceptions about dyslexia fuel student frustration and low self-esteem.
- Various assessments can identify characteristics of dyslexia.
- Parent knowledge and behavior are important to the success of dyslexic students.
- External and internal conditions may be risk or causative factors of dyslexia.
- Teachers can employ various strategies to assist struggling readers.

As indicated in the introduction of this chapter, struggling readers are those with a reading disability or learning difference who may be one or two grade levels behind

DIFFERENT READING STYLES AND ENVIRONMENTAL FACTORS

their peers. These children, who are in the lowest 20 percent of their class, experience difficulty decoding words successfully before or by first grade. Struggling readers come from all levels of social and economic environments. The student could be from a nurturing home that provides a stimulating educational environment or from an impoverished environment that provides little or no reading stimulation during the early years of life. Reading disabilities are either inherited or acquired through environmental circumstances. These different learners will need intensive services early on, including tutoring, to prevent serious reading problems later on. Every effort should be made to enhance reading skills during the early years, especially before third grade, so that these students are not mislabeled for special-education classes when their reading issues could be resolved with one-on-one or small-group direct instruction, using a strong cognitive base (e.g., Learning Rx).

Teaching Tips

Research various assessment tools for identifying struggling readers and intervention programs; conduct ongoing assessments; utilize various intervention strategies that accommodate the student's learning style; provide daily feedback. Based on your understanding of this chapter on different learners and/or struggling readers with different reading styles, respond to these salient questions:

1. What are common problems among different learners? How can you help struggling readers with different learning styles and backgrounds? Write up a sample strategy using a hands-on, multisensory approach.
2. What are some recommendations for modifying behavior of students whose behavior interfere with learning?

Suggested Websites

Listed below are some helpful websites for interventions and teaching tools that can help teachers, students, and parents who homeschool. These websites, which are concerned with literacy for different learners with special attention to the dyslexic learner (the struggling reader with hidden disabilities), address and describe learning differences and possible solutions.

Websites for Interventions and Teaching Tools

Brain Child
http://www.brainchild.com — Helps students "study better and score higher" with self-paced instruction on computers and mobile devices.

Learning Planet
http://www.learningplanet.com — Includes hundreds of learning activities, requires a paid membership to access.

Eduplace
http://www.eduplace.com — Includes textbook support materials for educators, students and families.

iTools
http://www.itools.com/research-it — includes tools for language, media, internet and money.

Intervention Central
http://www.interventioncentral.org — includes response to intervention tools and resources.

Suggested Readings/Resources

Boykins, A. W., and C. T. Bailey. 2000. *The role of cultural factors in school relevant cognitive functioning.* Report 43. Washington, DC, and Baltimore, MD: Howard University Center for Research on the Education of Students Placed at Risk, Supported by US Department of Education. Retrieved from www.CSOS.jhu1.edu.

Jensen, E. 2000. *Different brains, different learners: How to reach the hard to reach.* Thousand Oaks, CA: Corwin Press.

McEwan, E. K. 2002. *Teach them all to read: Catching the kids who fall through the cracks.* Thousand Oaks, CA: Corwin Press.

Moats, L. 2000. *Speech to print: Language essentials for teachers.* Baltimore, MD: Paul H. Brookes Publishing.

Payne, R. K. 2005. *A framework for understanding poverty.* Texas: aha! Process.

Tyner, B. 2004. *Small-group reading instruction: A differentiated teaching model for beginning and struggling readers.* Newark, DE: International Reading Association.

CHAPTER 3

The Educational Environment and Behavioral Issues

Chapter Subheadings
Organizing the Environment
Strategies for Bonding with Students
Dyslexia, ADD, and Related Behavioral and Learning Differences
Checklist for Setting up a Brain-Compatible Environment

OBJECTIVE
To demonstrate the role of an organized learning environment through examples of differentiated instruction that support learning differences and desired student behavior.

TERMS TO KNOW
Attention Deficit Disorder (ADD): commonly characterized by difficulty concentrating; individuals may be easily distracted and may require intervention in order to maintain acceptable behavior in school or on the job; may also complete projects of interest with commendations.

Attention Deficit Hyperactive Disorder (ADHD): commonly characterized by a constant state of anxiety and unpredictability; individuals may also be highly intelligent.

Bonding: an interactive strategy for developing a working relationship with students as well as within respective families.

Approximately 5 percent of students who have been diagnosed as struggling readers may also have behavioral issues that further complicate their readiness to master the complexities of reading. Therefore, a few fundamental discipline approaches will be discussed in this chapter that may require support from all stakeholders including parents and school and community leaders. For example, parents could be helpers in the classroom while also learning of better ways to reinforce concepts and provide support at home. If more children were succeeding with the support of parents, teachers, and school resources, there would likely be fewer times undisciplined behavior would appear in the classroom. Many experts say that when children are successfully engaged, discipline problems diminish or, many times, disappear completely.

This chapter will include some positive strategies that influence the behavior of students who are identified as struggling learners with behavioral issues. Students with disruptive behavior usually improve when teachers (a) plan engaging work with culturally relevant content, (b) provide clear directions, (c) model the process for the final product, (d) guide a lesson with whole class or small groups, (e) assign independent work, and (f) explain the evaluation process and expectations using a rubric describing what is expected at each stage of the lesson. Expectations should be clear, consistent, and firm. Also, teachers should accommodate students one-on-one if special needs are identified.

Organizing the Environment

Struggling readers usually have profound problems organizing and keeping up with materials and belongings. Having a place in the classroom for everything is very helpful for these different learners. This strategy helps build confidence in students and promotes the ability to remember and follow rules. It's also helpful to post rules and review them often and model expectations for students.

Consider the following classroom organizational tips at the beginning of school when everyone would like to know what is expected and where things go. These suggested organizational rules could be posted for the locations, things, and activities:

1. Teacher's desk: *State what is allowed and what is not allowed.*
2. Homework baskets: *Explain the inbox and the outbox.*
3. Supply box: *Identify where students store supplies that are used often* (e.g., scissors, paper, glue, extra pencils).
4. Routines for entering and exiting the classroom. Suggestion: demonstrate the process by "walking through" it with students.
5. Common problems and consequences (e.g., provide rules and consequences for students disrespecting the teacher or any one presenting in class, talking out without being recognized, getting out of their seats, or yelling for the

teacher or another across the classroom). Suggestion: create finger codes or signs to hold up.

Among strategies that could be employed for effectively managing student behavior are the following:

1. Follow through consistently; impose consequences calmly and quietly but ignore minor incidents and help other students to do the same.
2. Encourage students to take responsibility for managing behavior.
3. Redirect misbehavior in positive directions.
4. Preserve the dignity of the student. Struggling readers should not be compelled to read aloud in front of the class unless he or she made the request, even then, review the presentation privately to ensure student success.
5. Provide opportunities to earn free-time activities. Create opportunities for all students to earn points or incentives through various activities (be certain to have scissors, paper, glue, and extra pencils on hand).

The teacher sets the climate for the classroom. Bonding and establishing consistent respect from everyone is crucial. One of the most effective ways to bond with students is to attend events that students are engaged in, such as musical performances, sports events, and other programs. There are also widely accepted universal instructional strategies for the primary learning styles of struggling readers with related disorders that cause reading difficulties.

Sometimes children with language difficulties will also have an attention deficit disorder and attention hyperactive disorder known as ADD/ADHD. Susan Barton (Barton Reading & Spelling System), a national trainer on dyslexia and ADD, warns that a child can have a severe attention disorder that will prohibit the ability to concentrate on developing the complex science of reading. Often parents and teachers have reported situations where characteristics of dyslexia and attention deficit disorder overlap. The characteristics of ADD below may sound similar to some characteristics of dyslexia listed in chapter 5. If you know someone who has either set of these characteristics, similar instructional strategies can be used in most cases, although the causes of the characteristics are slightly different. For these learners, consistent routines and rules with fair consequences for breaking rules are important. They need an "in-control" teacher who can manage well. One word of caution, verbal threats have not been found to be effective. (These learners subconsciously visualize the consequences and work toward the consequences—be they good or bad).

Consider Mr. P., an example of an excellent teacher who did not recognize limitations. He had a class of twenty kindergarten students, the majority of whom were developmentally delayed or ruled as hyperactive. His kindergarteners filed in, greeted by their smiling teacher and the sound of cheerful music. Activities started promptly, including early bird activities. When it was transition time, the music changed, and the students knew what to do. For example, they would clean up quickly and move to the large group area. He would make positive comments about students who sat in their assigned colorful space or assigned workstation. Then, he focused immediately on that day's concept with things to see, do, touch, smell, taste, and/or hear. When new concepts were introduced, he would sometimes put on a bright yellow hard hat for *hard* thinking. If more than a few did not understand, he became the "confused slow learner" himself. Then student volunteers, one after another, had to teach him and make it plain. To keep the young "teacher" on track, Mr. P. would ask key questions, and the whole class got involved to help him "understand."

Having repeated answers from different ones provided the needed seven or more repetitions that most struggling readers need to ensure mastery. Incidentally, 75 percent of his students had been ruled "developmentally delayed" by the school's assessment team, which included a counselor. By the end of the school year, no one could identify which students in Mr. P's kindergarten class were developmentally delayed based on test performance. Children in his class wanted to be responsible, so they worked hard to learn what was expected. The teacher facilitated the learning process by stimulating the whole body: interacting, pairing students for small tasks, and competing in one-legged races on the playground to chart speed and measure space. The room was filled with interesting things to manipulate and form patterns: things to see and compare, hear and echo, taste and describe, and smell and identify. Rules for each workstation were reviewed periodically before groups were assigned routinely.

In a second-grade class of another teacher, student-group leaders were in charge unless help was needed. For example, assigned leaders knew to raise a red "help" sign when the group needed the instructor to stop, to raise a sign with a big yellow question mark if clarification was needed, or to raise a green sign when finished. As most teachers know, attitudes of the children, teacher expectations, and instructional styles vary from one class to another and from one grade level to another. This is especially true in middle and high school. Identifying the special interests of students and seeking ways to bond with them are prerequisites of teachers in the middle and secondary grades. Teachers in the upper grades have seen the significance of bonding with their students, especially those of diverse cultures.

During the 1980s, the work of A. Wade Boykin (1983) and an African-based research project conducted by Janice Hale-Benson were enlightening. Hale-Benson examined the outcome of African American culture on a child's intellectual development and learning style. It appeared that native African students and African American students had a commonality that may enlighten teachers of African American students in the United States. She observed that students did not perform as well in classes where the focus was primarily on content with little or no prior bonding (getting-to-know-you intros) in the teacher-student relationship. It was important for students to know *first* that the teacher cared, was fair and consistent, and had expectations and goals for the class. After studying the lifestyle of African students, Hale-Benson found that students whose teachers made an effort to *know* the students—their strengths, talents, and goals—scored higher on tests than those in other classes where the teachers made little or no effort to allow students to bond on a more personal level.

Boykin (1983) also recorded the African American learning styles in "The Academic Performance of Afro-American Children" and found similar learning patterns. He discussed three cultural themes: (1) communalism (need to connect in a support system type environment); (2) movement (dance and rhythm); and (3) verve (psycho-motor interactive learning) (321–371). In a later study, Boykin and Bailey (2000) provided a descriptive analysis of the influence of home environmental and cultural factors on the students' cultural orientation and learning preferences (17). Also, Covey (1997), international teacher and authority on effective leadership and family, found that he was most effective in his teaching career when he required his students to submit an autobiographical sketch for his files. Students were pleasantly surprised when he shared something that he knew about each one from time to time. He found that students performed better when he could personally relate to them during the course of the class. In summary, he explains from the point of view of a young person (student or family member): "I don't care how much you know until I know how much you care" (Covey, 1997, p. 157). These theoretical findings still hold true in the twenty-first century.

Similarly, W. Crockett conducted action research in 2004 at an urban middle school that reported difficulties getting 5 percent of their males engaged in the instructional-learning process. That relatively small percentage was disrupting the instruction for the other 95 percent. This action research was duplicated in a local school setting to validate his original research, which had been done in 1995 at Mississippi State University. The objective of the "Inbounds, Cognitive-Behavioral Counseling Model for Adolescent Males in the Middle School" was to work with school personnel (principals, teachers, and counselors) to identify academically promising middle-school students whose behavior inhibited their school performance. These students were exposed to twelve forty-five minute sessions of behavior management and modification training. Procedures for identifying and selecting participants for the In-Bound project were school based. Prospective project participants were referred by teachers, school counselors, and administrative staff. The project was designed not just for students who consistently exhibited negative and disruptive behavior but also for those who exhibited academic promise.

The purpose of this action research project was to motivate participants to display positive behaviors and attitudes that would enhance their academic performance. For the first step, ground rules were established for the sessions, and in the second step, students set consequences for anyone who violated the agreed-upon rules. During the eight weeks, the twelve young men learned to be attentive, cooperative, and responsible by being present for activities and, especially, present for school. After eight weeks, the documentation indicated significant improvement in the students' general conduct and classroom performance. Teachers discovered that spending some time one-on-one with students could diffuse their hostility. Bonding with students became a key to reaching some students.

Strategies for Bonding with Students

Jannie Johnson, a writer, journalist, and preventive counselor, has a unique way of dealing with young people. Her philosophy is to teach young people how to make wise choices early in order to prevent later unwanted behaviors and consequences, and she is most proud of her preventive counseling role. She is the founder of the Caring 'N Sharing School, in which she shares her proven strategies that have changed lives since 1988. Her focus is to "warn" and "prearm" children before they choose the undisciplined road to *nowhere special*. She teaches children to understand themselves first, know the truth about life, and hang on to those truths that are consistent and that will help them make the right choices. She trains her volunteer staff to internalize and implement strategies that are crucial in developing a working relationship with students and within their respective families.

She believes that "teachers should bond their relationship with the students by first, convincing them of their worth to self, family, school and community." Johnson is often contacted to help students with unruly behavior; however, her goal is to teach the principles of truth and life's lessons early to help prevent wrong choices that may lead to disruptive behavior. She shared the following sample cues and suggestions for teachers. Notice how she builds confidence while establishing high expectations.

Teacher says: "You can do this. I can help you. I know how to help you, but I need your cooperation to get this job done. I can't do it alone." Teachers may also adapt other positive statements during the class period:

1. Say: "Learning is a lifetime journey. We will take a few steps at a time—lesson by lesson, concept by concept."
2. Say: "Remember what we are learning today because we will have an oral review before the next lesson to see how much you have mastered." (Education is stacking the information in sequential or meaningful order.)
3. Say: "Try to remember three things, but be sure to remember one. This is how we will remember." (Use graphic organizers or first letters from familiar words to help students remember. For example, in music the spaces of the base clef spell FACE.)
4. Instructors should present the information in three different ways: Level I (easy), Level 2 (average), Level 3 (above average). To increase retention, engage at least three of the five senses in each lesson: see, smell, touch, hear,

taste. Now, the instructor should be ready to support, and the child should be in the mental state to learn.
5. Be consistent with your time, procedures, and expectations.
6. All along the way, convey belief that the child can master the learning goals.

The Johnson method is not as effective in large classes where disruptive students can feed off each other. If disruptive students have been identified and referred to her school, she schedules them individually or in small groups of six to eight. Like most experienced teachers, Johnson encourages teachers to bond with students especially in large classes. This can be done by using seating charts and assigning seats with name tags until the names and faces are mastered. Establish or post about five simple rules and routines on the first day of school. Walk and talk through the rules, practice the rules, write about the rules, and recite the rules. Review rules and consequences regularly, especially at the beginning of school and following school breaks and holidays. Let students know that when they break a rule, the consequence is their choice. Be consistent, be fair, and wear a businesslike facial expression until they have earned a smile or an approving gesture (e.g., high five, thumbs-up, etc.).

The rationale for alternative strategies to modify student behavior has been underscored in research studies. The National Institute on Health and Human Development (2003) reported that when students do not learn to read by third grade, many become behavior problems in the classroom. The study even indicates how predictions are made in the political arena regarding the number of jail cells to build based on the reading level and failure rate in third grade. Due to this lack of success in the early grades, approximately three million students drop out of school each year. Because they did not remain in school and prepare for a career, society will pay around $40,000 a year for those absorbed in the prison system. On the positive side, General Colin Powell, (Shuger, 2012) stated that the country could benefit from an additional $154 billion in estimated income earned over the lifetime of these millions of dropouts if they chose to be successful and productive. It is imperative, therefore, that teachers identify common learning differences in the classroom.

Dyslexia, ADD, and Related Behavioral and Learning Differences

Dyslexia is an inherited learning difference that may be observed or discovered through word perception, concepts, lexical patterns (letter combinations or morphemes of a language), and/or motor inhibitions. Dyslexia can also be acquired as a result of an accident that damages the brain or body. For example, a hand injury that has compromised fine motor skills may affect writing skills.

Causes of ADD/ADHD vary medically but generally it is inherited 75 percent of the time; 25 percent of the time it is acquired. ADD/ADHD is not acquired in the same way as dyslexia. There is usually a chemical imbalance that may need medical attention, while dyslexia is a neurological condition that is treated with brain-friendly therapy and routines. Mild cases of attention-deficit behavior may also be derived from mimicking behavior in the immediate environment.

In 2008, we attended training on the Barton Reading & Spelling System based on the Orton-Gillingham strategies for teaching struggling readers. Susan Barton gave her students permission to use information from her text, *Tutoring People with Dyslexia* (13–17), as long as it was properly documented, with the goal of helping struggling readers. In a supplementary fashion, she dedicated a day to addressing characteristics of ADD and drew parallels among those characteristics and those of dyslexia. In addition to the discussions on dyslexia, this section includes some information about ADD/ADHD—a closely related disorder that many times interferes with learning to read.

This brief discussion is by no means extensive in covering research and current information about ADHD, but information appearing in Exhibit 3.1 may enlighten some parents and teachers who may have been seeking approaches that could enhance what they currently know and do. Many times a dyslexic child will have some of these symptoms or the child with ADD will have dyslexic characteristics.

Exhibit 3.1: Attention Deficit Disorder/Hyperactivity Disorder

CAUSES		*Neuro-chemical imbalance*: The needed amount of Dopamine is not consistently delivered to the frontal lobes that control attention, focus, and logic. They have: • no control over their neurotransmitter delivery system • difficulty concentrating, and the more effort made seems to lessen the success level • no control over where the chemical imbalance may manifest itself (home, school, church, sport events, clubs, birthday parties, restaurants or wherever)
SYMPTOMS	1)	*Attention Deficit (or Attention Overflow)*. It is a deficit if the proper attention is not given to what should be the focus. But, more often it is diffusing the attention to too many things. Therefore, appearing highly distractible to the point of being overwhelmed and refusing to start on a given task. The individual: • is easily distracted by auditory or visual stimuli. • is even distracted by internal thoughts. • has difficulty with listening and taking notes at the same time. • is inconsistent in performance—can perform a task well today, but may have problems the following day or on tests.
	2)	*Disorganized*. May have a: • messy room, school desk, locker, notebook, and backpack. • difficult time scheduling homework or class projects
	3)	*Lack Effective Strategies*. Most ADD students don't know how to properly get attention and assistance so they often elicit the opposite of what they want or need. For example, they may need comforting, but try to get it by whining or showing aggression. The individual: • is not accepted by his/her peers, so s/he is less popular due to a lack of social skills. • is ostracized by their peers because of impulsively doing bad things such as grabbing things or hitting others. • often fails to understand social cues such as body language, jokes and idioms. • may become the loner or misfit who is teased, picked on or rejected by peers. Adults may accuse him/her of being lazy, stubborn, and a troublemaker.

Source: Barton, 2008, 1: 31–32; 1: 54–56.

Other symptoms of ADDHD that may be seen in behavior at home or in classrooms are termed impulsive behavior. Barton (2008) described these behaviors as follows:

1. impatient, may throw temper tantrums	9. does not appear to listen
2. poor visual-motor coordination	10. seldom finishes what is started
3. slow to complete work	11. seldom turns in homework on time, if at all
4. easily confused by instructions	12. wants center of attention; chronically restless
5. lots of careless errors and almost detest checking work	13. disturbed sleep patterns (night owl)
6. talks excessively; interrupts and forgets rules and blurts out answers	14. moody; excessive display of affection
	15. fail to anticipate consequences of actions
7. strong sense of justice/fairness	16. usually has lots of allergies
8. bossy; extraordinarily persistent	

Source: Barton 2008, 1: 32–33.

While most children may display these behaviors from time to time, children with ADD/ADHD go to extremes. They are in a constant state of anxiety and unpredictability. At school, they are often in trouble and sent to the principal's office for failure to follow rules or perform at expected levels. They tend to have an average IQ or the ability to do the class work but may engage in nonproductive work. They often develop emotional problems such persistent feelings of anger and anxiety.

Recent medical research on wellness reveals that ADD can be worsened by eating food with high levels of dyes and preservatives. This research found that natural foods, physical therapy from chiropractors, and/or adequate sleep can reduce many symptoms that would otherwise require strong drugs. To assist the child with focusing, several educational investigators and researchers have tried to tap into the complex brain and help identify dyslexia and related disorders. In addition to ADD/ADHD, below are some other related disorders to help identify symptoms that *are not* dyslexia (Barton, 2008. , 1:37)

Dysnomia or *dysphasia* is a word-retrieving deficiency that could be a symptom of dyslexia. Individuals having this disorder have difficulty retrieving words while speaking.

Dysgraphia is difficulty with the act of handwriting or writing the symbols in language. This could be caused by physical injury or an inherited inability to grip the pencil in the traditional way. When determining if it's a symptom of dyslexia, look for the following: (a) odd pencil grip, usually with thumb across top of fist; (b) inconsistency in letter formation, such as a mixture of uppercase and lowercase letters that may not set on the line; (c) inconsistent slants of tall letters; (d) odd use of space between words; (e) inability to copy from the board in class; and (f) learning to write cursive faster than manuscript. If an individual has difficulty *only* with the act of writing and has no problems with spelling, speaking, comprehension, copying, memory, or reading, he or she would be diagnosed as having *dysgraphia.*

Hyperlexia (also called Asperger's syndrome) is a multibehavioral condition that may include being an early talker but a late walker; being sensitive to sound; having social and physical behavioral differences such as flapping hands or wiggling fingers; and lacking eye contact, which may affect the way the child socializes, understands, and learns. It is somewhat like dyslexia in that both are characterized by average to above-average intelligence, but dyslexic students usually do not have abnormal behavior unless they have acquired it to draw attention to their needs.

Effective accommodations such as the ones above have been used successfully in the past decades. For instance, during the nineties there were trends to implement interdisciplinary teaching and thematic instruction. Interdisciplinary teaching was defined as the "cooperative effects around central themes that are relevant to the lives of students."

Cooperative learning came along during the same era with interdisciplinary teaching. Interdisciplinary teaching and cooperative learning are still practiced in the modern classroom where students are trained to serve their team members in given leadership roles (e.g., captain, monitor, recorder, reporter). Sometimes, the faces of cooperative learning, interdisciplinary instruction, Garner's (1999) interest group instruction, and pair-share collaborations can be seen in the much talked about *differentiated instruction* of the mid-2000s.

Marie Clay's *Reading Recovery Program* was one of the most effective one-to-one research-based intervention strategies practiced by trained teachers of struggling readers (Allen 1996). Teacher coaching was beginning to catch on as an effective innovation to replace team teaching. Other names for instructional paraprofessionals during the last decade of the 2000s included instructional specialists, learning specialists, certified tutors, tutors, interventionists, and all kinds of coaches—ranging from teachers to superintendents. Research-based interventions and coaching strategies began to be more in demand as school accountability and standards for student learning became paramount. *High-stakes testing* were the buzzwords, but effective school leaders required teachers to teach more than review test items and have students memorize facts. Students were expected to memorize and adapt the conceptual process. They also had to know how to apply the concept in a real situation or solve an assimilated problem. These higher-level thinking strategies were often too difficult for the struggling learner who had difficulty reading the directions.

Effective instruction for tactile learners, such as struggling readers with some characteristics of dyslexia, find that maintaining information in the long-term memory is more likely to occur when teachers use multisensory methods. In the upper grades or secondary school where students go to several teachers for different subjects, it is imperative that teachers collaborate in their planning so that there will be thematic instruction whenever possible. Teachers can also share effective methods similar to the ones previously outlined and those listed below in Exhibit 3.2.

Exhibit 3.2: Intervention Methods Effective with Young Children

Language-based interventions use pictures or video clips with phonics to learn letters and sounds (e.g. Between the Lions). After lunch, have students move to the letters in spelling words—bend down for all letters with a stem below the line, clap for each letter written on the line, and reach high for letters that extend high above the line. Fox example, spell S-p-e-l-l (Say "s"-clap, "p"—bend down toward floor, "e"—clap, "l" "l"—arms go up twice! and so on with all spelling words.

Reading and writing: Use fiction or non-fiction stories to spark discussions and responses. According to age or grade, have picture walks for young students or graphic organizers for older students and map story theme and other story elements.

Project-based learning: Problem-solving tasks should be incorporated into most lessons and should always align with the curriculum objectives. Projects should relate to real life situations when possible and applied to solve problems or explain phenomena.

Source: CORE 2000, chapter 13, 13.6.

Current research and federal legislation for special-education services guide the selection of intervention methods. The most effective interventions for dyslexic students are language based while incorporating multisensory teaching techniques and process-oriented strategies. The structure of written American English is best presented in a systematic, sequential, and cumulative design. A linguistic approach incorporating all aspects of language (phonology, morphology, semantics, and syntax) is essential to understanding the structure of language. If the teacher understands the structure, then the needed intensive and systematic phonics instruction can be provided to equip the student with the tools needed to master reading, writing, and spelling.

Dyslexic students can experience reading success in the regular classroom. The degree of success depends on the accurate assessment of reading behaviors and the effective instructional strategies tailored to the students' reading style. After mastering the alphabetic code, the next hurdle is developing fluency. Several strategies have worked with struggling readers. An interactive strategy mentioned here for working with fluency enhancement is adapted from Gail Adams and Sheron Brown's book, *The Six-Minute Solution: A Reading Fluency Program*. This strategy has been used by many teachers, even though the procedures may vary slightly. There are, however, many other effective ways to enhance fluency among struggling readers.

What follows is one of the fluency enhancement strategies that works. Using a timer, students take turns listening to each other read for one minute each day. They record the beginning times and ending times for each selected passage read for five consecutive school days. Students compare the first day with the fifth day. The paired students, when evenly matched, can record miscues and other reading errors on the duplicate reading monitoring form. *The Six-Minute Solution: A Reading Fluency Program* offers wonderful timed passages and graphs that can be used to monitor fluency among students of different reading levels (Adams and Brown 2004). The peer-teaching strategy is also used by many teachers to monitor written work, and to check math activities. This collaborative effort, of course, should follow a whole-group class discussion when concepts are explained and students are first guided through the process before working in pairs and working independently.

Checklist for Setting up a Brain-Compatible Learning Environment

Educators should ask themselves probing questions when setting up a brain-compatible learning environment. Are there opportunities for high levels of feedback and social interaction? (Language-challenged students can comprehend concepts better when steps are discussed orally before and after the final product.) Are demonstrations or models provided, especially for the visual-auditory-kinesthetic learners? (Most struggling readers and writers need to see and touch examples of what is expected.) Is the environment set up so that students can choose, for example, a supervised dimly lighted area of the room in which to work instead of the general well-lighted area? (Some students feel emotionally calmer and brain receptive in well-supervised, dimly lighted areas. Some teachers add soft classical music and large beanbags to respond to the natural senses.) Does the problem-based assignment have a built-in, rubric-type of assessment? (All kinds of learners appreciate and respond positively to opportunities for input, purposeful movement, and self-evaluation.)

Below are some recommended readings and online resources to apply in real classrooms and in teacher-training classes. The next chapter focuses on screening for strengths and weaknesses so that educators can design better instructional approaches—using best practices from research-based programs, online educational networks, and other media resources.

Summary of Chapter Points

- A variety of positive organizational strategies can deter disruptive behavior.
- Observations of student limitations are important for promoting learning and behavior.
- Bonding with students is key to address potential behavior issues.
- A brain-compatible learning environment ensures students are provided opportunities for feedback and social interaction and selecting classroom areas conducive for their unique characteristics and includes strategies for enhancing reading, writing, and fluency

---

Teaching Tips for Classroom Use

1. Students who are having problems in all subjects due to deficient language and reading skills can get rules from Fry's book on vocabulary and from websites about words and how the brain works. Go online or to the public library and read excerpts from Fry's book on vocabulary and Tyner's book on small-group instruction. With a partner or small-group assignment, create a lesson plan for a small group of struggling readers. Remember to pretest for the specific needs of your students before making plans.
2. Problem-based issue: You have an obviously intelligent student in your class. He has an above-average verbal vocabulary and explains new concepts with precision. However, he responds to stories and language arts activities as though he were from another planet. Prepare a lesson for your entire class of twenty elementary students and show how you will accommodate this student in the learning environment without the threat of failure.
3. Create areas in the classroom that match students' learning styles (i.e., listening, viewing, tactile centers) and have adjustable lighting and seating arrangements. Such arrangements may be more appealing to students who prefer lower lights or seating on a couch while completing a project. Providing opportunities for students to select appropriate comfort areas helps to promote positive behavior.

Suggested Readings/Resources

Asperger's Syndrome. (n.d.). Retrieve from http://www.learningdifferences.com

Covey, S. (1997). The 7 habits of highly effective families. New York, NY: Golden Books.

Eide, D. 2011. *Uncovering the logic of English: A common-sense solution to America's literacy crisis.* Minneapolis, MN: Pedia Learning.

Fry, E. B. 2004. *The vocabulary teacher's book of lists.* San Francisco, CA: Jossey-Bass Books.

Tyner, B. 2004. *Small-group reading instruction: A differentiated teaching model for beginning and struggling readers.* Newark, DE: International Reading Association.

CHAPTER 4

Literacy Screening Designed for Enhanced Instruction

Chapter Subheadings
Identifying Reading Styles and Addressing Reading Difficulties
Selected Best Practices and Strategies

OBJECTIVE

To present a screening instrument designed to identify reading behaviors and select best instructional practices.

TERMS TO KNOW

Auditory-linguistic behaviors: behaviors associated with listening as a preferred form of gathering information and communications; spoken and written comprehension may or may not be compatible.

Kinesthetic and tactile behaviors: behaviors associated with the sense of touch or hands-on for learning activities.

Literacy: the ability to decode, reproduce symbols, and interpret language within a given culture; adapting these skills sequentially in various contexts to gain meaning, communicate, and solve problems for productive citizenry.

Visual-spatial behaviors: behaviors such as sequencing based on visual characteristics and order within space.

School administrators and teachers are desperately seeking ways to help their struggling readers to succeed in reading. To address these learning differences with minimal cost, a screening instrument is provided in this chapter to help determine the dominant learning style of struggling readers. Many educators have established that most students have overlapping learning styles, but one is usually dominant (Carbo 2007). Strategies are then developed around the dominant learning style for that student. The checklist survey form included in this chapter was first used with students who had characteristics of dyslexia but had not been officially diagnosed as dyslexic. Initially, fifty survey forms were issued to teachers who only suspected that their students exhibited some characteristics of dyslexia. The results of this screening form were then compared with the findings of formal diagnostic assessments of students. It was discovered that the characteristics that determined the learning style using the screening instrument were consistent with the diagnosis made with the official diagnostic instrument. The process was repeated by comparing similar results of at least ten diagnosed cases of dyslexia. This screening survey form identified 95 percent of the same assumptions made by commercial instruments. The limitation of using the screening instrument is that it describes what has been observed by two or three people who have interacted with the student. Even though 95 percent of the cases matched the learning styles identified by the certified examiner, it is still recommended that official diagnoses be made for those who have profound characteristics of dyslexia. Mild to moderate cases could exhibit a few characteristics that could be supported in the classroom along with other struggling readers with similar weaknesses. These students could then be grouped according to similar accommodations needed. Severely dyslexic students may have limitations in all sections of the screening instrument. The student who is identified as dyslexic (which averages two students per every twenty in a given class) will need further assessments to determine the level of need and kind of services required, which is usually one hour of therapeutic intervention per school day.

Identifying Reading Styles and Addressing Reading Difficulties

If a student or students are not responding to the conventional interventions provided in the regular classroom, the survey instrument in this chapter may be useful to teachers and administrators in assessing the needs of struggling readers. The three-part form is designed to support teachers, counselors, and administrators by giving a profile of struggling students so that referrals to a teacher-support team will describe the kind of learners to be discussed. From this vantage point, suggestions, strategies, and interventions can be prescribed. The different reading styles will be addressed over the next three chapters, including classroom strategies and interventions that may be used to accommodate students' respective learning styles while they are learning to read. Many researchers have addressed this task before, and many have discovered that trying to isolate the characteristics of dyslexia is futile. As one school administrator stated: "Too many characteristics of dyslexia overlap with other reading disabilities, so why label the student as dyslexic? Let's just address the need because we have too many children who can't read and too few trained paraprofessionals to assist."

Therefore, the survey form encompasses and focuses on both the learning behavior of dyslexic students and on students who struggle to read due, primarily, to environmental circumstances. The teacher will want to recognize the characteristics of the learner in order to address the weaknesses. The survey form is recommended for grades two through eight, but it has also been used by high-school teachers. Whenever the characteristics are dichotomous, it usually shows that the student is obviously knowledgeable when answering questions orally but fails when responding to written questions. The causes may be due to fragmented recall or extremely poor handwriting or spelling. As one dyslexic adult ("Susan") explained, she could recall some of the information, but her metacognition (thoughts within her thinking) would dominate the main idea in the given text. She would connect self to text with experiences that came to her mind while writing and would respond to the text accordingly, but the response would be totally disconnected with what was discussed in the assigned text. Her teachers wondered how her intelligent oral answers were on target in the oral discussion but so unrelated when put in writing. Her handwriting did not translate her thoughts. In frustration and desperate to find a solution, the teacher asked Susan to read her own writing. Susan first stumbled over several words and then began to interpret what she had written. She did not read her writing and explained, coyly, that what she was saying aloud was what she intended to write.

The data sheet and *"Checklist for Reading Styles and Related Behavioral Differences"* (Exhibit 4.1) are designed to determine early learning styles and behaviors. Three sections of the checklist outline the specific characteristics of each behavior. Notice that the scale is from 1 to 5. When assessing the learning behavior, the number of checks under the 4s and 5s *only* need to be recorded; if *five or fewer* checks are in lower-numbered categories (1–3), this means the student has no significant weaknesses in these areas. On the other hand, if *six or more* characteristics are checked under either the 4s or 5s, that indicates the student's learning style should be addressed with strategies that are recommended following the checklist, and close monitoring should occur. If after six weeks of interventions no significant progress is made, then further testing is recommended. If the school or school district does not have certified personnel or a psychologist who can administer the necessary testing, the state department of education can be contacted for referrals.

Parents or guardians should be informed of the student's learning style or difficulty and why the student is being recommended for checklist screening and/or testing. Parents will also need to provide medical information in order to rule out acquired or existing medical conditions (e.g., birth defects, serious accidents, emotional or physical conditions that may influence the learning style). The information gathered should be recorded on the student data form and, by law, should be kept confidential. To ensure this, it is required to inform parents of the student's needs and get signed permission before screening or testing a student. This can be done in the form of a letter or special form to be signed by the parent or guardian, granting permission to proceed with the evaluation. (A sample letter to parents is in the Resource Section.)

This checklist form should be completed by at least two persons (e.g., teacher and parent or counselor and tutor) who have observed and worked with the student being screened. The totals in each section should then be compared for commonalities. If there are strong differences in the numbers, it may be necessary to have the student respond to the items in the form of an interview to determine the learning style or problem areas as perceived by the student. The checklist that follows begins with a student demographic profile and contains three sections: auditory-linguistic behaviors and visual-spatial behaviors.

LITERACY SCREENING DESIGNED FOR ENHANCED INSTRUCTION

Exhibit 4.1: Checklist for Reading Styles and Related Behavioral Differences

Instructions: The personal data included should be completed and treated as confidential information.

Biographical Data:

EXAMINER: _____ **Date:** _____

1. _____ 2. Gender: F/M _____
   Last name   First Name   Middle

3. _____ 4. _____
   Student I.D. Number   Contact Number

5. _____
   Date of Birth: Month/Day/Year

6. Has a grade been repeated?   Yes ☐   No ☐   If yes, list grade(s) _____
   Current Age   Grade Level

7. _____
   School Name:

8. School Address: _____ School Phone Number: _____

9. Parent or Guardian of minor _____
   Address

10. _____
    Home Phone Number:

11. _____
    Emergency or Cell #

12. Has examinee been tested for academic or medical reasons?   Yes ☐   No ☐
    If yes, attach results of tests and health/medical history that influence the outcome of assessment.

13. Has examinee applied for special accommodations or special education services?   Yes ☐   No ☐
    If yes, briefly explain the outcome

    _____
    _____
    _____

Please check the items below that best estimate the length of time you have observed or known the student:

☐ Less than 3 months   ☐ 3 – 6 months   ☐ 6 months – one year   ☐ More than one year

Note: This checklist has been completed for training purposes. Please assess the student screened and determine if he or she has characteristics of dyslexia. A sample letter to parents is provided in the Resource Section.

Exhibit 4.1 Checklist for Reading Styles and Related Behavioral Differences (Continued)

Directions: Use the checklist below to rate the extent to which the examinee demonstrates each behavioral characteristic in academic and social environments. The checklist is divided into three sections that are often observed among students who are being screened for characteristics of dyslexia. The examiner should carefully and objectively underline each item that best represents the characteristic exhibited by the examinee. Please rate each behavioral statement based on the frequency of occurrence using the following scale: (1) never (2) seldom (3) sometimes (4) often (5) always.

Section I: Characteristics of Auditory – Linguistic Behaviors		
The Examinee		
		Scale
1.	seems to have the intellectual ability/potential to develop reading, writing, and	1 2 3 4 5
2.	prefers academic and leisure activities that involve listening skills.	1 2 3 4 5
3.	remembers better when things are discussed and shown what to do.	1 2 3 4 5
4.	experiences difficulty in remembering information (e.g., appointments, class	1 2 3 4 5
5.	follows simple oral directions well, but is easily distracted.	1 2 3 4 5
6.	tends to have difficulty following multi-step directions.	1 2 3 4 5
7.	knows materials one day, but forgets it the next unless it is repeated several	1 2 3 4 5
8.	has difficulty writing the letters of the alphabet in sequence without a model	1 2 3 4 5
9.	may have difficulty memorizing and retaining words for spelling tests	1 2 3 4 5
10.	has difficulty naming the vowels	1 2 3 4 5
11.	has difficulty using the correct short vowels in spelling words	1 2 3 4 5
12.	has extreme difficulty spelling high-frequency/sight words (e.g., they (thay),	1 2 3 4 5
13.	may have difficulty reading basic sight words or sequencing letters (i.e. left for	1 2 3 4 5
14.	has difficulty decoding (sounding out) words using phonics skills	1 2 3 4 5
15.	has difficulty blending letter sounds	1 2 3 4 5
16.	comprehends stories or text better when read aloud by others	1 2 3 4 5
17.	has poor oral reading skills—slow and laborious	1 2 3 4 5
18.	reads below grade level, but may memorize recorded poems or dramatic	1 2 3 4 5
19.	may have difficulty recalling everyday words in conversation.	1 2 3 4 5
20.	takes wild guesses to complete a statement when right word does not come	1 2 3 4 5
	Count the number of 4s and 5s ONLY. Place Total here →	

Exhibit 4.1 Checklist for Reading Styles and Related Behavioral Differences (Continued)

Section 2: Characteristics of a Visual Spatial Behaviors	
The Examinee	
	Scale
21. has difficulty lining up and/or sequencing math problems.	1 2 3 4 5
22. still reverses letters and/or numbers after primary grades (e.g., b and d; 15	1 2 3 4 5
23. has difficulty determining hand preference	1 2 3 4 5
24. is unable to keep place on the page while reading	1 2 3 4 5
25. uses finger or pencil frequently to maintain place during reading in upper	1 2 3 4 5
26. has difficulty copying information from board assignments or chart	1 2 3 4 5
27. mixes capital and lower case letters when writing (e.g. doG, cAt)	1 2 3 4 5
28. forms letters with different line patterns or lengths and slants	1 2 3 4 5
29. has illegible, "messy" handwriting	1 2 3 4 5
30. fails to notice details in surroundings	1 2 3 4 5
31. has difficulty reading and using maps	1 2 3 4 5
32. has difficulty remembering directions when walking or driving	1 2 3 4 5
33. may spell better orally than in writing	1 2 3 4 5
34. spells with correct letters, but in the wrong sequence (e. g., left, felt)	1 2 3 4 5
35. has difficulty describing visual characteristics of familiar people and places	1 2 3 4 5
37. has an awkward, tight, fist-like pencil grip when writing	1 2 3 4 5
38. masters, orally, class lessons/concepts taught, but may test poorly on written	1 2 3 4 5
39. has repeated a grade one or more times (repeated once, check 4; two or	1 2 3 4 5
40. has benefited from traditional reading programs with basic reading strategies	1 2 3 4 5
Count the number of 4s and 5s ONLY. Place Total here →	

Exhibit 4.1 Checklist for Reading Styles and Related Behavioral Differences (Continued)

Section 3: Characteristics of a Visual Spatial Behaviors	
The Examinee	
	Scale
41. may have loud sub-vocal sounds during silent reading	1 2 3 4 5
42. has a better memory of what is said than what was read	1 2 3 4 5
43. has difficulty structuring time and managing time	1 2 3 4 5
44. tends to freeze or stare in space during tests, especially timed test	1 2 3 4 5
45. May be rigid and inflexible; needs structure	1 2 3 4 5
46. Is easily distracted	1 2 3 4 5
47. Makes frequent negative comments about school	1 2 3 4 5
48. makes negative comments about reading, writing and/or spelling activities	1 2 3 4 5
49. seems to ignore or has difficulty understanding non-verbal social cues and	1 2 3 4 5
50. makes insensitive and blunt remarks that sometimes repel friends	1 2 3 4 5
51. tends to freeze or become frustrated if asked to present/perform before an	1 2 3 4 5
Count the number of 4s and 5s ONLY. Place Total here →	

Note: No two dyslexic persons are exactly alike. The section with the most checks is considered to be his or her learning style. Record the total of items checked for each section. If there are ties or a balance among the three areas, continue as directed below providing only totals of 4's and 5's.

Learning Style (Check one)

Section 1: 1s___ 2s___ 3s___ 4s___ 5s___ Total of 4s and 5s ___

Section #1 ___
AUDITORY LINGUISTIC

Section 2: 1s___ 2s___ 3s___ 4s___ 5s___ Total of 4s and 5s ___

Section 3: 1s___ 2s___ 3s___ 4s___ 5s___ Total of 4s and 5s ___

Section #2 ___
VISUAL SPATIAL TACTILE

Section 4: 1s___ 2s___ 3s___ 4s___ 5s___ Total of 4s and 5s ___

Record the sum of the section with the highest number of 4s and 5s.___

Section #3 ___
AUDITORY-LINGUISTIC AND VISUAL/SPATIAL

If the examiner has observed and checked a total of **six or more** statements from the "4" and "5" categories, the examinee has characteristics that are consistent with dyslexia and further testing should be considered.

Other observations: Please list below other known areas of strengths, talents or weaknesses of this examinee that are not listed in the survey.

©2009 Developed by Mamie B. & Walter L. Crockett. All rights reserved. No part of this publication may be reproduced or published without written permission of the authors.

©2009 Developed by Crockett, M.B., & Crockett, W.L. All rights reserved. No part of this publication may be reproduced or published without written permission of the authors.

After assessing all the ratings, make the final determination of learning style. If the parent is satisfied with the screening results but not satisfied with the proposed accommodations, it may be necessary to recommend the student to the school's counselor for comprehensive testing. Most school districts are not required to test for dyslexia but will screen for dyslexic characteristics and determine if comprehensive testing is necessary. The primary concern for most teachers of struggling students is that adequate resources and accommodations are available. With high expectations and student mastery of core standards, paraprofessionals are invaluable human resources to monitor learning performance and progress.

Selected Best Practices and Strategies

Handwriting and spelling can be separate behavioral characteristics. During the early stages of writing, for example, children are beginning to develop small muscles in the hand; therefore, one can expect to see large letters perfected before small lowercase letters. Most moms of preschoolers and teachers of prekindergarten classes provide spaces for the young prewriters to write. As most young moms know, if a space is not provided, there will be wonderful notes proudly written with illustrations on a wall in the family room! The nerves that are stimulated in the hand go through the arm and shoulder directly to the brain to register the operation. Many opportunities should be provided to develop small nerve-laden muscles for both the small and connected large muscles.

The following sample activities will enhance tactility, visual acuity, and spatial development:

- Scribble on large paper, or erasable boards.
- Use etching pads.
- Use old-fashioned coloring books connected to stories read.
- Create letters and objects with nontoxic modeling clay or dough.
- Trace letters (e.g., letters of his or her name, family members, and classmates) using colored sand, salt, or grains of rice.
- Overlay letters to be mastered with a twelve-by-twelve-inch section of window screen. (This could be donated from the local lumber company, but cover edges carefully with duct tape before using.)
- Use embroidery stencils to safely overlay letters to provide tactile experiences.

Even though video games involve eye-hand coordination, recent studies indicate that these games do not stimulate the senses that enhance long-term memory. In other words, they do not grow dendrites, the sprouts that develop in the brain when learning takes place. However, games can be created that will stimulate senses and assist struggling readers. An example is the Blend Switch Game. The directions in Exhibit 4.2 are simple.

Exhibit 4.2: Directions for the Blend Switch Game

1. Copy and cut out blend words and glue on index cards. (The cards can also be laminated for repeated use)
2. Shuffle cards.
3. Deal each player 7 cards.
4. Place remaining cards in the middle of players. Turn over one card.
5. The first player must put down a card that has the same blend as the card faced up. (EXAMPLE: If the card on the table says black, the player could play bland or blunt. The player reads the words as they place the card down.
6. If the player does not have a card with the same blend, the player can:
   (a) Place a switch card down and change to another blend (example: Player says, "Switch to flip", and places the flip card down)
   (b) Player can pick from the deck. If he has a card he can play, he can use it during his turn. Before the game begins decide whether the player continues to pick from the deck until he gets a card he can play or if the player will pick one card per turn.
7. The first player to use all of his or her cards wins.

Instructions: Cut cards for each set of blends and SWITCH cards. Use the words below or any other blends you may need to reinforce.

black	bland	Blab	blot	blank
blend	blunt	Blink	Blob	block

blast blend blink blob block
blend blunt flap flip flop
flag flat fleck flint fling
flint flock floss flub slab
slam slap slat sled slab
slid slim slip slit slob
slot slug slant plan plot
plop plot plug plum plus
plank plant plump pluck plunk
SWITCH SWITCH SWITCH SWITCH SWITCH
SWITCH SWITCH SWITCH SWITCH SWITCH

The next chapter proposes some strategies and approaches that teachers can use to accommodate students with the primary learning differences described in the three broad areas.

Summary of Chapter Points

- A screening instrument can identify the dominant learning style of struggling readers.
- Three learning styles are most frequently found among students with five or more characteristics of dyslexia.

- Regular home activities provide opportunities for developing small muscles used for writing.
- Activities should be designed to enhance tactile, visual, and spatial development.

Teaching Tips

- Work with the teachers in your school to do this exercise: each of you has been appointed the lead teacher in a failing school. More than 25 percent of the students are performing two grades below grade level in reading. Form a group of four and discuss with your group how you might address this problem. Record your strategies, and then, research best practices from this chapter, referring to the suggested readings below or from online resources. Record specifically the steps and procedures your group will take to screen for the kinds of reading needs and how you will proceed to help raise the reading scores of the lowest quartile. Meet with the other groups of teachers to share and discuss your strategies.
- Use informal instruments to identify students' learning needs. A combination of assessments will yield information that will help you to make more informed decisions for selecting appropriate interventions.

Suggested Readings

Dean, C., R. Hubbell, H. Pitler, and B. Stone. 2012. *Classroom Instruction that works.* 2nd ed. Denver, CO: McREL (Mid-continent Research for Education and Learning).

Jensen, E. 2000. *Different brains, different learners: How to reach the hard to reach.* Thousand Oaks, CA: Corwin Press.

Reeves, A. 2011. *Where great teaching begins, planning for student thinking and learning.* Alexander, VA: ASCD (Association of Supervision and Curriculum Development).

CHAPTER 5
Learning Styles and Concomitant Instructional Strategies

Chapter Subheadings
Student Learning Styles and Suggested Instructional Strategies
Differentiated Instruction and Accommodating Learning Differences
Modifying Instruction for Hard-to-Reach Students with Reading Difficulties
Universal Strategies for Different Learners

———

OBJECTIVE
To present best instructional practices for specific learning styles and hard to reach students.

TERMS TO KNOW
Accommodation: a definite procedure to adjust learning environments to address learning difficulties or to solve a problem.

Direct instruction: a highly structured teaching approach designed to accelerate the learning rate of students who can benefit from prescribed lessons based on prior assessments, response to interventions and observations.

Hard-to-reach students: struggling students who have lost confidence in their ability to learn due to (1) lack of reading readiness skills; (2) little exposure to good reading models; (3) learning English as a second language; (4) socioeconomic conditions; (5) professionally diagnosed behavior issues, or a combination of these characteristics.

According to one dyslexic student's perspective, "Many teachers just don't get it. They are teaching with enthusiasm to other students, and they are getting it, but my teacher doesn't know that I am faking it. I can't remember what word I said a few minutes ago. I have to fake it so others won't know that I sometimes get simple things wrong. My words just come out different from what I am thinking."

Many struggling students wish they could digest quickly what the teacher said or decipher what is written on the board. A dyslexic struggling reader commented, "I try hard to recall what you just said and directions about what everyone is expected to do. The words written in black on the white board seem to move around just when I think I know what the words mean! Everyone has started the board work, and some have almost finished. You think I am sitting here, wasting time, but I am trying so hard to sort and arrange the words to make sense and get the answers right! I feel like a ball lost in tall grass."

These statements describe the dilemma of struggling dyslexic students when trying to complete board work in the regular classroom. There are three major learning styles that are often found among students with five or more characteristics of dyslexia: auditory-linguistic, visual-spatial, and a combination of auditory-linguistic and visual-spatial. These were discussed in chapter 4 and sorted by sections in a survey form to be used with struggling readers. This survey form has evolved over a ten-year period in a school system of 31,000 students where 85 percent of the thirty-eight elementary principals were convinced by student performance data that a significant portion of their students had a reading disability called dyslexia. The other 15 percent remained in denial or minimized the reading deficiencies, citing environmental influences (such as poverty), disruptive behavior, lack of quality instruction, and/or limited teacher resources as the causes.

Student Learning Styles and Suggested Instructional Strategies

This section is devoted to identifying behaviors that are characteristic of the three major learning styles demonstrated by struggling dyslexic students. Suggested instructional practices are provided based on the observation of students. Exhibit 5.1 contains this information.

Exhibit 5.1: Student Learning Styles and Suggested Instructional Strategies

Student Learning Styles If the examinee:	Recommended Instructional Strategies
1. seems to have the intellectual ability/potential to develop reading, writing, and spelling skills [but does not succeed with general class instruction].	Consider investing in *Kurzweil 3000* to assist in developing these skills. It could be worth the approximate $2,000 that may help change a child's life. (View online at http://www.kurzweiledu.com/) Note: Usually children with learning differences have *silent questions* about their inability to perform on the expected grade level, especially when they are making obvious efforts. Children should be encouraged to develop their *weaknesses* through identified *strengths*.
2. prefers academic and non-academic activities that involve minimal listening skills.	Give auditory directions with visuals and hands-on activities so that what is said is easier to understand and remember. (Parents or school could invest in Franklin KID-1240 on Amazon to assist with small groups. Costs around $30.)
3. remembers better when shown what to do.	Demonstrate the board work or assignment. Provide study sheets and outlines (in larger than 12 point font size). With older students, use NCR paper when making assignments, so that they can have a copy for notes.
4. experiences difficulty in remembering information (e.g., board work, homework assignments, etc.)	Many learning different students have difficulty holding in the mind information from the board long enough to reproduce the board item on a sheet of paper. Instead, it is recommended that the same assignment is provided in large print on a sheet of pastel colored paper.
5. does not follow oral directions well.	For younger children, class and/or homework assignments, for example, may be written on colored paper and issued to struggling learners. Older students may request a review and/or master quick note taking skills.
6. tends to have difficulty following two or three-step directions.	Introduce students to graphic organizers that outline sequence and have students to number what comes first, second, third, etc. Place visual reminders on desktop.
7. knows materials one day, but forgets it the next.	Children with inherited brain differences should have concepts repeated at least 12 times in about seven different ways before dendrites grow in the brain. One resource that may also help is *Ghotit Dyslexia Assistive Technology* that can network to all schools **free** with a sign up cost of $14.99.

Exhibit 5.1 Student Learning Styles and Suggested Instructional Strategies (continued)

Student Learning Styles	Recommended Instructional Strategies
If the examinee	
8. has difficulty writing the letters of the alphabet in sequence without a model.	Begin with letters of his/her name and those of close relatives and friends. Remind student of those persons when reciting the letters. Then, review sequence of letters as a daily warm-up activity. (For example, say: "What letter comes before"f"; after "s?")
9. reverses letters and/or numbers.	If the child is in kindergarten or first grade, it may be a visual maturity issue. But, after late first or second grade strategies to help with retention should be used. Allow children to use graph paper and colored pencils to write problems.
10. has difficulty naming the vowels.	Mnemonics and creating jingles help with memory. See Resource section with various ways to memorize concepts.
11. has difficulty using the correct short vowels in spelling words.	Phonemic awareness is a listening skill that may take extra time for some different learners. Teach the open and closed syllable types and/or consonant-vowel-consonant words (CVC/c-a-t) and the seven types of syllables. Use repeated practice.
12. has extreme difficulty spelling high-frequency/sight words (e.g., they (thay), was (wuz).	Write the part that gives the most trouble larger than the rest of the word. /W/ can be heard in was, but the "as" part is not phonetic. Therefore, write words so that the tricky letters stand out, e.g., wAS.
13. has difficulty reading basic sight words.	Use word patterns and word families. Have students draw the words or draw what comes to mind.
14. has difficulty decoding (sounding out) words using phonics skills.	Use the same strategy as #12. Teach spelling rules for students to adapt when needed.
15. has difficulty blending letter sounds.	Demonstrate blending by mixing colorful juices to make punch. (Sample it!) Then, show how letters need our tongue and teeth to blend sounds of the letters. (Tasting and connecting meaning will help grow dendrites.)
16. comprehends stories or text better when read aloud by others.	The majority of children with characteristics of dyslexia, or related reading disorders, may comprehend better when stories are read aloud. Therefore, experts encourage accommodations that include recorded answers using a tape recorder.

Exhibit 5.1 Student Learning Styles and Suggested Instructional Strategies (continued)

Student Learning Styles	Recommended Instructional Strategies
If the examinee:	
17. has difficulty writing the letters of the alphabet in sequence without a model.	Begin with letters of his/her name and those of close relatives and friends. Remind student of those persons when reciting the letters. Then, review sequence of letters as a daily warm-up activity. (For example, say: "What letter comes before"t", after "s?")
18. reverses letters and/or numbers.	If the child is in kindergarten or first grade, it may be a visual maturity issue. But, after late first or second grade strategies to help with retention should be used. Allow children to use graph paper and colored pencils to write problems.
19. has difficulty naming the vowels.	Mnemonics and creating jingles help with memory. See Resource section with various ways to memorize concepts.
20. has difficulty using the correct short vowels in spelling words.	Phonemic awareness is a listening skill that may take extra time for some different learners. Teach the open and closed syllable types and/or consonant-vowel-consonant words (CVC/c-a-t) and the seven types of syllables. Use repeated practice.
21. has extreme difficulty spelling high-frequency/sight words (e.g., they (thay), was (wuz).	Write the part that gives the most trouble larger than the rest of the word. /W/ can be heard in was, but the "as" part is not phonetic. Therefore, write words so that the tricky letters stand out, e.g., wAS.
22. has difficulty reading basic sight words.	Use word patterns and word families. Have students draw the words or draw what comes to mind.
23. has difficulty decoding (sounding out) words using phonics skills.	Use the same strategy as #12. Teach spelling rules for students to adapt when needed.
24. has difficulty blending letter sounds.	Demonstrate blending by mixing colorful juices to make punch. (Sample it!) Then, show how letters need our tongue and teeth to blend sounds of the letters. (Tasting and connecting meaning will help grow dendrites.)
25. comprehends stories or text better when read aloud by others.	The majority of children with characteristics of dyslexia, or related reading disorders, may comprehend better when stories are read aloud. Therefore, experts encourage accommodations that include recorded answers using a tape recorder.

Exhibit 5.1 Student Learning Styles and Suggested Instructional Strategies (continued)

Student Learning Styles	Recommended Instructional Strategies
If the examinee:	
26. has an awkward, tight, fist-like pencil grip when writing.	Have student to practice the "pencil pinch" (pressing the thumb and point finger together forming a bird's beak). Then gently slide the pencil in with the middle finger closing in to support the "bird's beak." Assist student in moving hand to paper and practicing writing. (Get additional support from http://www.cdl.org).
27. masters lessons and concepts better when presented and discussed orally, but still test poorly on written tests.	Consider modifying the testing process. If accommodations are not approved due to ineligibility rulings, document and discuss the learning style with the local Teacher Support Team and/or conference with parents. (If grades do not represent ability, recommend comprehensive testing.)
28. has repeated a grade one or more times.	Retention is not a recommended, research-based intervention method. A few exceptions are social maturity (age difference and performance level are two or more grades below that of peers) or behavioral immaturity due to health issues causing developmental delays physically and intellectually. http://www.advocatesforchildren.org/pubs/retention.html; http://www.fairtest.org/care/boston%20dropouts.html.
29. has not benefited from traditional reading programs with basic reading strategies.	There are several intervention methods that have been effective with struggling readers with dyslexic tendencies. Examine Orton-Gillingham based programs like *Lexia* for younger students and *Language!* for older students (4th grade up). If budget is limited, contact the *Texas Scottish Rite Hospital* about the *Dyslexia Training/ Literacy Program*. Copyright is waved, therefore, groups or schools can purchase and copy about160DVD lessons taught by a certified linguist for a fraction of the cost of similar multisensory programs. Based on quantity, most corresponding student workbooks and teacher guides are about $10 each.
30. has difficulty structuring time and managing time.*	Encourage parents to get an alarm clock for getting to school on time, and for home-school activities and events. Color-code notebooks and subject tabs so that time is not lost looking for assignments or reporting assignments. Try to avoid *rushing* this kind of mind.

*Listed out of sequence from Section 3, but combined for convenience to apply and adapt strategies. Other behaviors in Section 3 may be modified on a case-by-case basis with the support of the school's counselor.

Exhibit 5.1 Student Learning Styles and Suggested Instructional Strategies (continued)

Student Learning Styles	Recommended Instructional Strategies
If the Examinee:	
31. has an awkward, tight, fist-like pencil grip when writing.	Have student to practice the "pencil pinch" (pressing the thumb and point finger together forming a bird's beak). Then gently slide the pencil in with the middle finger closing in to support the "bird's beak." Assist student in moving hand to paper and practicing writing. (Get additional support from http://www.cdl.org).
32. masters lessons and concepts better when presented and discussed orally, but still test poorly on written tests.	Consider modifying the testing process. If accommodations are not approved due to ineligibility rulings, document and discuss the learning style with the local Teacher Support Team and/or conference with parents. (If grades do not represent ability, recommend comprehensive testing.)
33. has repeated a grade one or more times.	Retention is not a recommended, research-based intervention method. A few exceptions are social maturity (age difference and performance level are two or more grades below that of peers) or behavioral immaturity due to health issues causing developmental delays physically and intellectually. http://www.advocatesforchildren.org/pubs/retention.html; http://www.fairtest.org/care/boston%20dropouts.html.
34. has not benefited from traditional reading programs with basic reading strategies.	There are several intervention methods that have been effective with struggling readers with dyslexic tendencies. Examine Orton-Gillingham based programs like *Lexia* for younger students and *Language!* for older students (4th grade up). If budget is limited, contact the *Texas Scottish Rite Hospital* about the *Dyslexia Training/ Literacy Program*. Copyright is waved, therefore, groups or schools can purchase and copy about 160DVD lessons taught by a certified linguist for a fraction of the cost of similar multisensory programs. Based on quantity, most corresponding student workbooks and teacher guides are about $10 each.
35. has difficulty structuring time and managing time.*	Encourage parents to get an alarm clock for getting to school on time, and for home-school activities and events. Color-code notebooks and subject tabs so that time is not lost looking for assignments or reporting assignments. Try to avoid *rushing* this kind of mind.

*Listed out of sequence from Section 3, but combined for convenience to apply and adapt strategies. Other behaviors in Section 3 may be modified on a case-by-case basis with the support of the school's counselor.

Differentiating Instruction and Accommodating Learning Differences

In the process of differentiating instruction and incorporating suggested best practices, teachers may consider the basic principles of cooperative groups. Some teachers find it helpful to color-code the roles students have in groups. The colors are brain friendly and help the visual learner remember their assigned responsibilities.

Cooperative Groups

The formation of cooperative groups has been modified in several ways since the initial inception of these groups during the eighties (Johnson, Johnson, Nelson, and Skon 1981). Historically, each lesson began with the teacher instructing and modeling; that remains as the first step in the strategy. Second, the children in the group work together to master a teacher-assigned task. The grouping strategy could be heterogeneous or homogeneous and range from two to five students working together. Third, children work on individual assignments within the group-assigned task so that each part is essential to the overall team's work. They then report and share their findings or learning. The team is graded by the combined average of all members of the group. Slavin (1991) discovered that cooperative learning methods increased a student's self-concept and social skills along with improved academic performance. This method is highly recommended for struggling students who need to feel a part of a group that is socially and academically compatible. The group discusses the assignment before the final presentation, helping each member to feel confident about the presentation. It is also recommended that a student who is not severely dyslexic serve as the reporter since some students "freeze" in front of an audience or class. Depending on the teacher's preparation for such assignments, the experience can be a positive or negative experience.

Identifying Cooperative Groups

When implementing cooperative group practices, several steps may be involved. A suggested practice is to make labels or signs for each of the roles described below, writing the title and its responsibilities on colored paper corresponding to that role. Give each group member the paper identifying and explaining his or her role. Read aloud and explain all the roles to the group so that all clearly understand what is expected during any given assignment. Provide copies of all the assigned roles to the leader.

> **Leader (red):** The leader may review the directions aloud to the group. The leader should be able to assist group members in understanding and completing the work.

Illustrator (blue): The illustrator may draw an image of what is being discussed in a story or draw a graphic organizer to illustrate points to be presented by the group.
Recorder (green): The recorder writes whatever the group is assigned. He or she may also assist the word wizard in recording definitions.
Reporter (orange): The reporter is the speaker for the group. The reporter may, for example, interview the main character in a story for the group or read the written response of the group as directed by the teacher.
Word wizard (purple): The word wizard will mark difficult words in the reading assignment and write them in a word bank or journal. Later, the word wizard will use a dictionary to define the difficult words.

Frequently, in the regular classroom, dyslexic children have been misunderstood or, often, inappropriately mislabeled. By now, it is hoped that most myths and misunderstandings have been erased or obliterated.

The screening instrument described in chapter 4 has also been used by teachers to document the steps taken to modify instruction for different learners. Additionally, an accommodation checklist (Exhibit 5.2) can be an effective tool to further document current strategies used to help struggling readers on a daily basis. Teachers should make every effort to adapt report cards to reflect accommodations. A modified form used by one school to record accommodations made for targeted, struggling students appears in Exhibit 5.2. Teachers can modify the form to meet the respective needs of their students,

All teachers will not feel comfortable accommodating and adapting lessons to match the learning style of a student when the majority of the class has to conform. "Accommodating students with special needs is not fair to my other students!" remarked a frustrated but sensitive teacher. This attitude can be rebutted with this question: would it be fair to have a physically handicapped child in leg braces compete in a foot race with a child who has normal legs? Teachers can be fair, but the students cannot always be treated the same.

Exhibit 5.2: Accommodation Checklist

Student Name: _____ **Date:** _____
Grade Level: _____ **School Year:** _____
Teacher Name: _____
School Name: _____
School Address: _____

Instructions: Check all that best describes the student's accommodations.
- ___ (1) Test read orally for student
- ___ (2) Test explained to student in detail
- ___ (3) Assignments taped or copied for the student
- ___ (4) Instructional material altered or changed to meet student's needs
- ___ (5) Content material re-taught
- ___ (6) One-to-one instruction provided as needed.

Support Codes for Student Accommodations:
LS-Learning Support provided for student   IST-Intervention Support Team
RS-Remedial Services   TD-Teacher-Directed Support

Below is a checklist of special instructional accommodations provided based on identified student learning styles behavioral differences.

Subject	Support Code	Accommodations	Support Code	Accommodations	Support Code	Accommodations	Support Code	Accommodations
READING								
WRITING (LA)								
MATH								
SPELLING								
SCIENCE								
SOCIAL STUDIES								
HEALTH/ (PE)								
OTHER								

Modifying Instruction for Hard-to-Reach Students with Reading Difficulties

Often students begin thinking of ways to distract the teacher and peers after third grade when fundamental decoding and reading skills lessen in scope. In other words, before third grade, students *learn to read*. After third grade, students *read to learn*. Whenever students fail to master basic reading skills by third grade, one in eight will catch up and read on grade level (Juel 2001). Therefore, it is imperative that external stimulation and personal interest somehow merge for struggling readers who have lost confidence in their ability to read.

Following a poor performance, one struggling reader shouted out, "I hate this class! I'm not learning anything in here anyway." He rhetorically asked, "Who wants to read all the time?" In this situation, the teacher was smart and didn't embarrass him in front of the class; rather, she paused and later asked to speak with him privately. The conversation went something like this.

> *T: Raymond, it seems you have strong feelings about this class. What bothers you the most?*
> *S: I am just not learning anything. Look at this paper. I didn't get but two questions right out of twenty.*
> *T: It seemed that you understood the story when we discussed it in class, so what gave you problems later?*
> *S: It's hard to explain. It seems that everything gets jumbled in my head, and what I think is right for one question is not. Words gets turned around, and some of the words in the questions are hard to read, so I guess at what the words say.*
> *T: Raymond, you seem to get along well with Stephen, right?*
> *S: Yes.*
> *T: Would you be willing to partner with him in reading so that you can support each other during class assignments?*
> *S: Yes, that would help. And, Teach, I apologize for the things I said about class.*
> *T: Apology accepted. Remember, Raymond, I am here to help you, not to embarrass you or any other student for what you don't know. If you are not learning in the way I teach, help me to teach the way you learn.*

Sample Procedure
In modifying instruction for her struggling readers the teacher first proceeded to review assessment of the fifth-grader for reading weaknesses and strengths. Partner reading was used first when the chosen passage was repeated for a school week. One partner listened and timed the reading of the other. They then exchanged roles, using a one-minute timer to record their speed and accuracy. At the end of the week, the beginning time was compared to the ending time to determine the rate of improved accuracy and fluency.

Implementation

When implementing partner reading, we recommend choosing an interesting short passage that meets the criteria of leveled reading material. Student peers should be on approximately the same reading level but not necessarily have the same reading difficulty. Generally, students should be able to read at least twenty lines without error. If more than two words are missed within twenty lines, reconsider the choice of passage. The teacher may use a handout similar to the one in Exhibit 5.3 to assist in the peer evaluations. There should be one sheet for each partner to record progress.

Read-alouds were also initiated in modifying instruction to model fluency and prosody. At least twice a week, the teacher chose passages from leveled chapter books for the class to participate in *choral reading*. These strategies provided an opportunity for struggling readers to develop a feeling of self-confidence while hearing difficult words read accurately without personal embarrassment.

Choral reading is a strategy that is similar to choral singing. Everyone reads aloud together the same passage or poem. For poems, smaller groups within a class can be assigned to read certain lines or stanzas. When struggling readers experience success and realize that the teacher is truly interested in their success, the so-called hard-to-reach students become success stories. They no longer feel alone in their struggle.

Exhibit 5.3: Peer-Partner Reading Record Form to Enhance Fluency

Reader_____ Date_____

Listening Partner_____

Passage Used_____ No. of words_____

Day 1: Beginning time_____ Ending time_____ Difference_____

Day 2: Beginning time_____ Ending time_____ Difference_____

Day 3: Beginning time_____ Ending time_____ Difference_____

Day 4: Beginning time_____ Ending time_____ Difference_____

Day 5: Beginning time_____ Ending time_____ Difference_____

Compare the *Beginning time in Day 1* with the *Final time on Day 5*. Difference?____

This should be the best time among all the days timed. Partners should comment on the daily progress with this individualized record sheet and filed in assigned folder:

1) Reads more smoothly: ___Yes ___Somewhat ___Not yet

2) Reads with more expression: ___Yes ___Somewhat ___Not yet

3) Knows more words and reads accurately: ___Yes ___Somewhat ___Not yet

4) Stops properly for punctuation: ___Yes ___Somewhat ___Not yet

Comments:_____
_____

Teacher's name: _____
Class:_____

Form inspired by Archer, A. L., M. M. Gleason, and V. Vachon. 2005. *Reading Excellence: Word Attack and Rate Development Strategies (REWARDS)*. Longmount, CO: Sophris West. This company is a resource for offering strategic processes, materials, and Blackline Masters that teachers have permission to use.

Universal Instructional Strategies for Different Learners

In the early 2000s, when the dyslexia initiative was born in a local school district in Mississippi, there was a great need for resources to use with these brilliant students who could not read. In 1996, the Learning Disabilities Association (LDA) posted online Universal Instructional Strategies that could serve as tactics for teaching dyslexic students along with a teacher checklist addressing the three major types of dyslexic learners: auditory-linguistic, visual-spatial, and a combination of auditory-linguistic and visual-spatial. The association stated that this "checklist of behaviors is offered for classroom teachers (elementary and secondary levels) to use in determining behaviors characteristic of dyslexic functioning in their students" (LDA 2008, 1). The checklist is not included here, but some of the strategies were helpful in the initial project of that school district. Some of the strategies have been adapted here to further its original purpose and appear in Exhibit 5.4. Many of the strategies have been replaced with other language-based technological strategies. Nevertheless, many of the universal instructional strategies are just that—universal. The collective listing in Exhibit 5.4 is presented as yet another resource for teachers as certain learning needs remain constant. Hopefully, teachers will find the one link that a certain student may need if he or she is not responding to given interventions.

Exhibit 5.4: General Instructional Strategies to Enhance Learning

1. Provide background experiences for the students prior to having them read about specific topics. This will serve to heighten motivation to read while clarifying information
2. Make raised letters by allowing white liquid glue to dry in the shape of desired letters and words. Students can feel the letters and words by tracing over the dried glue. Letters are also effective tactile reinforcements if made from sandpaper, velvet, wood, or aluminum.
3. Incorporate sustained silent reading in your instructional program. When you also use this time to read silently, your students will come to realize that you really value reading.
4. On occasion, give students your test questions before they read a specified selection. This technique will provide the students with a clearly defined focus for reading.
5. Use creative dramatics. By combining creative dramatics with reading, students will better understand the story's sequence, plot, character relations, and so on.
6. Have the students create a newspaper. Various columns, such as a feature section, weather, or cartoons, can reflect students' divergent talents and

interests. Students can dictate their material to you if they cannot write it themselves. This information can be photocopied and used as a rich source of reading materials. The newspaper can also be sent home so that parents can become more fully informed about what is happening in your classroom.

7. Some students will require extrinsic motivation beyond verbal encouragement. Having students keep track of the books they read can be highly motivating.
8. Have the students use cursive script in writing assignments. (It is more difficult to reverse the letter pattern in cursive writing than in manuscript printing.) This strategy will encourage more muscular power control in the hand and thus a more distinctive tactile/motor pattern for each letter.
9. Provide meaningful drill practice of vocabulary words only after the word has been identified in the context of a sentence that the student understands.
10. Give special recognition to students who use above grade-level words/vocabulary in oral and written responses.
11. Have students form questions from a published author of stories. Advanced students may create questions from subtitles in an elementary science chapter on birds. (e.g. subtitle, "Birds That Cannot Fly" The question is, "Which birds cannot fly?")
12. Let students on occasion prepare their own quizzes to test the reading material.

Source: Adapted from *Learning Disabilities Association* (2008).

Students with hidden disabilities experience frustrations similar to those of a physically handicapped child in a foot race against a peer who is not handicapped. In response to these frustrations, some act out while others do not and instead patiently try to understand the lesson. We hope some of these suggestions will make the teacher's task a little easier when trying to meet the needs of diverse learners—both those who act out so that others will not discover their disabilities and the quiet patient ones, who also deserve to be educated like all others in the class. The next chapter takes into consideration instructional strategies that could be used in teaching spelling as a threshold to reading challenges of different learners.

———

Teaching Tips for Problem-Based Learning

1. Discuss with the class the kinds of discipline problems that have been observed or reported in schools today. Have an assistant principal come and speak to the class about the social and academic challenges faced on a daily basis.

2. With permission from a local elementary or middle school teacher, have class partners plan a visit to observe a class that has no discipline issues, and a teacher who has poor management styles. Prepare five questions to help guide the visit. (Caution: Students should not interrupt the instructional process.)
3. Cross-check appropriateness of instructional strategies through using an accommodation checklist. Forms that record tasks attempted and accomplishments achieved are useful for charting the daily progress of accommodations.

Summary of Chapter Points

The focus of this chapter was to synthesize common characteristics of struggling readers with different learning styles and with extenuating circumstances and propose abbreviated strategies. Strategies were provided to help modify learning behavior and present resources to assist students who have difficulties with (a) concentration (easily distracted); (b) erroneous perceptions of symbols (letter and number patterns); (c) retention of learned concepts; (d) memorizing sight words and spelling words; (e) memorizing multiplication tables with sequence of mathematical steps; (f) responding in writing to reading assignments; or (g) maintaining a high self-esteem and confidence in *knowing*. Furthermore, we suggested using appropriate assessment instruments to record the level of competence and weaknesses of targeted students so that necessary accommodations can be created.

Suggested Readings

Allen, N. M. 2012. *When teaching gets tough: Smart ways to reclaim your game.* Alexandria, VA: ASCD.

Dean, C., B. E. R. Hubbell, H. Pitler, and B. Stone. 2012. *Classroom Instruction that works.* 2nd ed. Denver, CO: McREL (Mid-continent Research for Education and Learning).

Fisher, D., and N. Frey. 2010. *Guided instruction: How to develop confident and successful learners.* Alexandria, VA: ASCD.

McEwan, E. K. 2002. *Teach them all to read: Catching the kids who fall through the cracks.* Thousand Oaks, CA: Corwin Press.

Mendler, A. 1999. *Work more successfully with difficult-to-reach students! Practical strategies for increasing your effectiveness with difficult-to-reach students.* Bellevue, WA: Bureau of Education & Research.

Tyner, B. 2004. *Small-group reading instruction: A differentiated teaching model for beginning and struggling readers.* Newark, DE: International Reading Association.

CHAPTER 6
Instructional Spelling Strategies to Enhance Reading and Writing

Chapter Subheadings
The Reciprocal Skills of Reading and Writing
Connecting the Five Components of Reading
The Decoding Spelling Continuum with Grade-Level Expectations
Traditional Best Practices: Revisited

OBJECTIVE
To demonstrate the relationship between skills of reading, spelling, and writing and corresponding instructional strategies.

TERMS TO KNOW
Phonemic awareness: conscious understanding that spoken language is composed of speech sounds (phonemes).

Reading: the ability to interpret and understand codes and words of a given language and communicate that through oral and written expressions.

Reciprocal Teaching: the instructional process that incorporates the reading strategies of predicting, questioning, clarifying, and summarizing.

INSTRUCTIONAL SPELLING STRATEGIES TO ENHANCE READING AND WRITING

Spelling is the act of using letters or symbols in a specific pattern to form words or to communicate meaning. Many individuals can read words without being able to spell them. Knowing how to read and spell most words is what most literate people have accomplished. However, misspelling high-frequency words that may not be phonetic—such as *want, was, they, two*—in a letter of application for a job could pose a problem.

Many individuals misspell a word occasionally but seldom misspell high-frequency words. It is acceptable to use word codes on social networks such as in texting friends, but it is unacceptable to misspell words of any kind in an application for employment. Forty-seven percent of Americans cannot successfully complete a job application without some assistance in reading and writing. Writing, in this instance, requires communicating accurately and effectively. A case in point: one employer read a cover letter of an applicant. There were several spelling errors. The employer discontinued reading the letter, and the attached résumé never saw the light of day. Spelling is essential in communication. If a prospective employer looks at a letter filled with spelling errors, most times the attached résumé will not be seriously considered.

Also important is the selection of words in a given language used by an individual to communicate meaning and understanding. Spelling and vocabulary work together to determine the level of literacy and communication skills. Therefore, it is perceived that reading and writing are reciprocal.

Literacy is the ability to decode and read print in a progressive intellectual manner to gain meaning, communicate, and solve problems. The United Nations Educational, Scientific and Cultural Organization defines literacy as the "ability to identify, understand, interpret, create, communicate, compute and use printed and written materials associated with varying contexts" (UIS-AIMS and Literacy Assessment n.d.). Educators and researchers have studied spelling and reading from different perspectives. Eide reminds us that English orthography (alphabetic written symbols) is often described as inconsistent and illogical (Eide 2011, 11). But some literacy experts defend the structure of the English language. Other scientific studies of the English language support the premise that English orthography is a structured and predictable system. The process of spelling words is mastered through understanding a predictable progression of phonemes, syllables, and morphemes that are rule governed and can be explained in terms of etymology (the historical origins of words), semantics (word meaning), and phonology (sound structure) (Glaser and Moats 2008, 16–17; 70–73).

The premise further implies that formal spelling can affect the efficiency and quality of written work. Spelling skills also enhance reading and writing skills. For example, fluent spelling skills, including an understanding of the encoding process, can immeasurably improve the mechanics of reading, writing, and computation. Formal spelling can affect the efficiency and quality of reading and writing skills. Comprehensive literacy development is foundational in the education of a child. Therefore, English orthography, including fluent spelling skills, requires an understanding of the encoding process, which can immeasurably improve the mechanics of reading, writing, and computation.

Initially, this chapter began by defining and describing the complexities of literacy including spelling, reading, and writing. Later, the collaborative concepts are extended to the expected skills that should be taught and mastered during the early grades (prekindergarten through third grade) and the upper grades (fourth grade and up). Literacy development is foundational in the education of a child. During the early cognitive developmental stage, a child may be able to understand meaning but unable to speak, read, or spell the words communicated. This is known as the *preverbal stage*. During story hour, "Alexis," age two, can be directed to go to a nearby table and "bring the red storybook" and will understand what she is being asked to do without being able to say those same words. Apparently, she has knowledge of color (red) and two key objects (table and the book). During a subsequent story hour, she may understand how to browse and select her favorite storybook from among other book choices. Her perception of "book" has broadened. A few years later, Alexis attends preschool, and her teacher asks students to share something about their favorite book. Alexis's prior experience with books has prepared her to boldly share her favorite red book, *Little Red Riding Hood.*

After sharing stories and discussing various literary materials during the early years, students may be directed to write in their journals. Kindergarteners usually write phonetically. If they have been exposed to books and hearing stories, the word scribbles may look like this: TH BK I LIK TH MOS IZ TH 3 BS. The first evidence of orthographic knowledge is invented spelling. The child understands that words are made from sound and that these sounds can be printed by using letters. These letters become words if placed in a pattern that follows the alphabetic principle. Interpreted, the scribble reads "The book I like the most is *The Three Bears*."

Most parents can remember teaching their three- or four-year-old child to print his or her name. The letters probably evolved from large lines and disjointed strokes on large lineless white paper (or on a chalk board) to legible uppercase letters on lined paper. Later, lowercase letters were added to the process. The child's name is frequently his or her first sight word. It may or may not be based on traditional phonics.

Elementary spelling rules sometimes are difficult for teachers to apply. For example, following the civil rights movement of the 1960s, some African Americans wanted to disassociate themselves from the names given to their forefathers by slave owners. Some who had no true family names created names that were totally original, using sometimes part of a family name with a new middle name. Many times the names were not phonetic but somewhat followed English alphabetic principles. For example, one girl liked the name of a flower, chrysanthemum, and wanted her newborn sister to have that name. The mother, a teacher, agreed and decided to modify the name to make it more phonetic for the child's sake—maintaining the *k* sound without the *ch* spelling. The letter *h* was dropped, and thus, Crysenthia! Like this mother, numerous parents manipulate letters and sounds to create one-of-a-kind names. Doing this may have helped some children gain phonemic awareness at an early age, while for others, it may have taken them a little longer to decipher their own names. Nevertheless, these young ones were exposed to letters and sounds and perceived that somehow they form words.

What role does phonemic awareness play in learning to spell? According to renowned author J. Richard Gentry, phonemic awareness is the ability to segment the speech sounds into words. Segmentation of sounds is a part of kindergarten and first-grade spelling. This awareness forms part of the underlying knowledge source of how the alphabetic system works, how the spelling system works, and how the decoding system works. There is no question about the role of spelling in literacy development. If a child does not know how the alphabetic system works, then he or she will not be able to use it to spell and communicate.

The Reciprocal Skills of Reading and Writing

Research has indicated that there are various reasons why some children between kindergarten and third grade do not learn to read at the same rate and approximate time as their peers. An equal amount of research supports the notion that children learn to read in different ways with different orientations and motivations. Before determining why some children miss the peak time of learning to read, let's define reading. How do scientifically based research and experts define reading?

Generally, reading can be defined as the ability to interpret codes and words to form an understanding of a given language. The online modern dictionary *Wikipedia* explains broadly the meaning of reading and the complex process as follows:

> Reading development involves a range of complex language underpinnings including awareness of speech sounds (phonology), spelling patterns (orthography), word meaning (semantics), grammar (syntax) and patterns of word formation (morphology), all of which provide a necessary platform for reading fluency and comprehension. (Wikipedia 2011, 3)

In other words, reading is the ability to interpret and understand codes and words of a given language and communicate that through oral and written expressions.

Through the years, we have come across several perspectives on reading. Marie Clay (1991, 6) says, "Reading is a message-getting, problem-solving activity that increases in power and flexibility the more it is practiced. In layman's terms, it is a tool, a skill, ability and a process."

If we view reading as a tool, it is similar to other tools, such as a pencil or keyboard. As a tool, reading can help in responding to written tasks, operating computers, texting on cell phones, and manipulating iPads. As a skill, reading is like typing: one can get better at it with continual practice. In typing, your fingers are guided to the letters and locations on the keyboard. With practice, the fingers and brain become one and master the keyboard. As a result, typing fluency comes. This is the same manner in which the reader's eyes connect with the brain during frequent practice; eventually the individual becomes fluent a reader. The more you read, the better you get at it. Reading comprehension is the final broad skill of understanding what you read, and it usually takes place after fluency.

First, the student learns letters, then letter sounds, and finally that certain sounds form words. If the student does not connect these concepts, the teacher should be able to determine why, for example, a kindergartener, age five, is unable to name the letters of the alphabet. It may be that the child has missed school far too many days to keep up. Also, there could be home conditions, school conditions, or an inadequate literacy environment (Samuelsson and Lundberg 2004). The child could be alert but lack school-readiness experiences. If the latter is the case, remediation and intervention strategies should begin immediately. It is imperative that children understand the reading codes as soon as possible.

However, it is a different process if the child comes from an ideal learning environment—lots of family attention, and broad exposure to the world—but still cannot grasp the connection among letters and their forty-four different sounds. The inability to identify and associate letters and sounds is what Samuelsson and Lundberg (2004) brought forth in their study to be the new argument for emphasizing phonological deficits as the core component in defining dyslexia. Therefore, this chapter incorporates core strategies of spelling from the Consortium of Reading Excellence (CORE 2001, 2008) and structural spelling strategies from the Orton-Gillingham (International Dyslexia Association 2000) alphabetic principles so that the best of researched-based practices are outlined to support struggling readers with the characteristics of dyslexia.

Phonemic awareness is the first of the five components of reading and probably the most important prerequisite to later reading success. Phonemic awareness is the ability to associate, apply, produce, manipulate, and combine the smallest units of sound (phonemes) in various ways to understand and form words. To master these skills, parents and teachers must expose the students to a variety of auditory tasks, including listening to stories, matching and rhyming sounds, segmenting and combining sounds, and clapping syllables. Evidence of understanding letter-sound relationships among consonants and short vowels may be prevalent for 80 percent of a class, but some struggling readers will not be able to associate basic letters and sounds. Therapeutic, systematic, multisensory approaches are required for the other 20 percent. That means, if one strategy does not work, the teacher should try another from a repertoire of accumulated strategies and accommodations (CORE 2008, 186).

Understanding the letter-sound patterns of high-frequency words, for example, may not match the forty-four letter sounds of the alphabet. That can be a challenge for struggling readers. Several approaches have been used successfully with different learners, and many are matched with these diverse learning styles in chapter 5. The chart in Exhibit 6.1 provides a list of words that young writers are expected to frequently use. When students have profound deficiencies in phonemic awareness, these words are often mastered to some degree by looking at the beginning letter or the shape of the word. Sometimes the words are miscued because there is not a thorough understanding of letter sounds.

To help young writers or reluctant writers get started, we have provided phrases that have been recommended to help students start sentences, extend sentences, and add ideas within stories. These phrases are included in Exhibit 6.2 for early and advanced grade levels. Additionally, the Blend Switch Game (see Exhibit 4.2) can assist in meeting this objective. As noted by experts with years of experience, encouraging students to read at least thirty minutes a day will increase overall vocabulary that is crucial to writing proficiency.

Exhibit 6.1: Word Bank for Young Writers

A, a	B, b	C, c	D, d	H, h	I, i	J, j	K, k	L, l
about	back	called	dad	her	if	jump	keep	land-
after	black	came	dear	here	I'm	just	kind	large
again	be	can	did	high	in		knew	last
ab.	bear	car		him	into		know	leave
also	because	cat		his	is			left
always	bed	children		hold	it			let
am	been	color		home	it's			light
an	before	come		horse				like
and	best	could		house				little
another	better			how				live
any	big							long
are	bit							look
around	book							lot
as	both							love
ask	boy							
at	brother							
away	but							
	by							

Exhibit 6.1 Word Bank for Young Writers (continued)

M,m	N,n	O,o	P,p	R,r	S,s	T,t	U,u	V,v,W,w
mad	near	off	people	ran-	said	take	under	very
made'	need	oh	place	really	saw	ten	until	walk
make	never	old	play	red	say	ten	up'	wanted
man	new	on	please	ride	school	than	upon	warm
many	next	once	put	right	see	that	us	
may	mice	one		room'	she	the	use	
me	night	only		run	should			Y,y,Z,z
mean	no	or			sister	their		year
men	not	other			small	them		yes
mice	now	our			so	then		yet
mom		out			some	there		you
money		over			something	these		you
more					sometimes	they		young
morning					soon	thing		your
most					spring	think		zipper
mother					start	this		zoo
much					still	thought		
my					summer	three		
					swim	through		
						time		
						to		
						together		
						told		
						too		
						took		
						tree		
						tried		
						two		

Exhibit 6.2: Jump-Start Young Writers with Phrase Writing

Grades 1-2	
saw a cat	came up to
at home again	a tall girl
as soon as	a big house
stand on the	find a rock
in the box	look at that
upon a time	is my mother
the first one	run out of
because it was	at school today
made me mad	with the people
could I go	all last night
in the book	I think that
into my room	on the back
begin to say	animal in the zoo

Connecting the Five Components of Reading

Again, what is reading? Simply stated, *reading is the ability to interpret codes and words to form understanding of a given language.* The process engages five reading components: phonemic awareness, phonics, vocabulary, comprehension, and fluency.

Phonemic Awareness

To connect the five components, books with key phonemes have been listed in Exhibit 6.3. Students using story books can see a practical application, association, and combination of phonemes.

Exhibit 6.3: Phonemic Awareness and Early Vocabulary Development
   Word families used in nursery rhymes
   "Bees": ay, may, hay
   "The Boy in the Barn": ay, hay, away
   "Curly Locks": ine, mine, swine
   "Five Speckled Frogs": og, rog, log; ool, cool, pool
   "Georgie Porgie": ay, play, away
   "Hey Diddle Diddle": iddle, diddle, fiddle; oon, spoon, moon
   "Hickety, Pickety, My Black Hen": en, hen, gentlemen; ay, day, lay
   "Hickory Dickory Dock": ock, dock, clock; ive, five, hive; ine, nine, fine
   "Humpty Dumpty": all, wall, fall
   "Hush-a-Bye Baby": all, an, fall
   "I'm a Little Teapot": out, out, spout, stout
   "Jack and Jill": ill, Jill, hin; own, down, crown

"Jack Be Nimble": ick, quick, stick
"Knick Knack Paddy Whack": ee, three, knee; ive, five, hive; ine, nine, shine; en, ten, hen, eleven, heaven
"Little Bo Peep": eep, peep, sheep
"Little Boy Blue": om, horn, com; eep, sheep, asleep
"Little Jack Horner": horner, comer
"Little Mouse": ouse, mouse, house; eal, steal, meal; out, about; un, fun, run; eep, creep, peep
"Little Sally Walker": est, west, best
"Mary, Mary, Quite Contrary": ary, Mary, contrary; ow, row, grow; ells, shells, bells
"Mockingbird": ing, ring, sing; brass, glass
"Monday's Child": ace, grace, face; ing, giving, living; ay, day, gay

Phonics

To be a successful reader, students need to understand the alphabetic principles and the alphabetic sounds that make up words. As students develop a higher level of awareness, they begin to understand how the general system works—how the letters of the alphabet can be rearranged to make forty-four sounds and create words (see list in Resource Section). Consequently, while children are learning the letters of the alphabet, they should also understand that particular letters form a pattern. When these sounds are blended, they create words. Words are then arranged into sentences to communicate meaning, which is the beginning of reading.

Vocabulary

There is no question about the role of spelling in literacy development. If a child does not know how the alphabetic system works, then he or she will not be able to use it to spell and communicate. Research says a preschooler usually has a vocabulary of about three thousand words, and the number doubles—and, for some, triples—each ascending year. Vocabulary is the heart of language. The student needs to understand the language of the classroom; otherwise, there will be difficulty in following directions, as well as problems with interpreting oral and written class assignments.

Common word identification and pronunciation can be achieved through working with word parts and understanding them. Vocabulary development strategies should be grounded in orthographic knowledge—understanding spelling patterns. Rules of spelling also should be introduced gradually so that vocabulary will grow simultaneously through personal experiences and understanding. Pronouncing big words can be enhanced by memorizing definitions of prefixes and suffixes and knowing how to attach them to root parts.

Comprehension automatically improves when older students can read multisyllabic words more fluently. Activities to improve reading and enlarge vocabulary encourage the following:

1. Have students learn to read prefixes and suffixes separately as well as the root word, and then read the parts together to form multisyllabic words.
2. With the students, look up the multisyllabic words in the dictionary to learn where the accent is located in the word. Teach that the accented syllable is usually the one with the baseball-bat-like mark. Sometimes there are two such marks in a word. In such cases, the larger or darker accent mark is the primary accent and the smaller or lighter one is the secondary accent with less stress. Demonstrate reading a multisyllabic word with the accent mark and have students, especially tactile learners, stamp their feet when they see the accent mark: for example, for com-pre-*hen*-sion, students would stamp on *hen*.
3. Word sorts are great reinforcement activities for struggling readers. Have students sort by rime patterns (ending of words), such as *-ake*, *-ble*, *-sion*; by sound, such as the long *e* in h*ea*t and ch*ie*f (this can be more difficult than simple patterns because the sound could be different in spelling); by tricky words and irregular words separately, such as *want, have, was*; and by pictures, which can help older struggling readers and visual learners to recognize beginning sounds and consonant sounds.
4. Play word hunt with students. In word hunt, students find word patterns in a reading assignment, such as a story. For example, have students make a list of words with common onsets: words with the same beginning sounds up to the vowel, such as bat, boat, bike.
5. Creating poems with words is also a way to engage students in other content areas. Introduce students to found poems. This is a free verse form where students create a poem by using specific parts of speech from a story or nonfiction passage. The subject of the found poem should reflect the original story or passage read, as in the example below, derived from "Jack and the Beanstalk."

Jack, beans, cow, sale
Beanstalk, golden hen
Englishman, Bread, Giant
Jack.

Comprehension

Reading comprehension is the broad skill of understanding what you read. How the student learns to decode and understand language depends on his or her learning style and the preparation of the teacher.

The previous word list in Exhibit 6.1 provides a widely accepted benchmark school word identification and vocabulary development list, and chapter 6 outlines the general sequence of expected spelling skills by grade level that lead to necessary encoding skills for reading. For additional multisensory methods and strategies, review the online and printed resources provided in the Resource Section.

Fluency
Fluency is the bridge between decoding and comprehension. It is sometimes a predictor of failure or success in mastering the science of reading through alphabetic codes and text comprehension. Being fluent in reading builds self-confidence and should be established early and fostered along with other talents. The down side is that if students do not succeed in establishing necessary skills for reading, they are more likely to become grade repeaters and potential dropouts.

Exhibit 6.4 is the actual text presented to a dyslexic student and the student's interpretation of what was seen when asked to read aloud appears in Exhibit 6.5.

Exhibit 6.4: Actual Text Presented to a Dyslexic Student

"Come on," said Betsy. "We have to
pick up this corn. We don't have
another can of popcorn."

Exhibit 6.5: Dyslexic Student's Description of Text

"Comeo		n." saidb	y. "We ehav		ets	eto
		r	egon" not			
di	cku l	o n.	W	thavea her	pth	sc
		fqodc	cano orn."			

(Thanks to R. D. Lavoie, Eagle Hill School for sharing.)

Struggling readers who may be dyslexic or have related disorders should be taught based on individually identified phonological weaknesses. These skills should include teaching how to (a) decode words accurately, (b) increase reading rate, (c) practice recognizing word parts and words automatically, (d) increase reading rate while maintaining accuracy, and (e) practice reading with prosody, that is, fluency and appropriate expressions (CORE 2008). Teaching fluency is difficult for both the teacher and the learner when decoding is weak; however, there are strategies educators recommend.

Considering that 80 percent of all words have one or more affixes, one fifth-grade teacher used fifteen minutes of several reading blocks and followed these steps in teaching multisyllabic words to her struggling readers:

1. Using an overhead projector, introduced common prefixes and suffixes.
2. Directed students in thinking of words and finding other words in the newspaper with common prefixes and suffixes.
3. Selected a group of prefixes to define and pronounce.
4. Selected a group of common suffixes to define and pronounce.
5. Pulled multisyllabic words from a reading selection. Discussed and circled the prefixes and suffixes with class.
6. Underlined the vowels in all syllables of the word.
7. Read the word by syllables.
8. Read the whole word and confirmed its pronunciation with the class, and allowed time for questions and clarifications.

Affixes can be collected or identified from reading assignments of the students as well (see Exhibits 6.6 and 6.7). Then, when a list of affixes is acquired, the teacher can write the affixes on a chart or use an overhead projector so that the entire class can see the list. The students are led to read the affixes quickly and accurately. Common suffixes should be presented, pronounced, defined, and repeated within the context of a sentence to help students develop understanding, fluency, and word meaning. Common prefixes are presented in Exhibit 6.6.

Exhibit 6.6: Common Prefixes

Prefixes	Meanings	Sample words and definitions
auto-	self; same one	automobile – a vehicle driven by oneself auto pilot—a plane flying by itself
bi-	two, twice, once in every two	bicycle –vehicle with two wheels, bicolor—two colors
dis-	do the opposite; not	disagree to have a different opinion disappear—to stop being seen
ex-	from, out, out of, away from	exhale—to breathe out exit—to go away from
pre-	earlier, before, in front of	prepare—to get ready earlier preview—to see something before
sub-	under, lower than	subway—underground train submarine- an underwater boat
re-	again, back, backward	repeat—to say it again rewind—to wind something backward

Some teachers also review closed and open syllables within this lesson so that the struggling readers can readily apply word skills in pronouncing syllables within multisyllabic words. For example, *pre-* is an open syllable. An open syllable ends in a vowel or the vowel stands alone and the vowel sound is long (it says its name), as in *prE*. In a closed syllable, like in the prefix *sub-*, the vowel is either in the middle of two consonants or the syllable begins with a vowel but ends in a consonant; in closed syllable, the consonant always closes the door on the *right* side of the vowel. In closed syllables, the vowel is short, as in the following words: apple, egg; Indian, oxen, umbrella.

Common suffixes should be presented, pronounced, defined, and repeated within the context of a sentence to help students develop understanding, fluency, and word meaning. Exhibit 6.7 contains some common suffixes that can boost word knowledge and reading fluency.

Exhibit 6.7: Common Suffixes That Boost Word Knowledge and Reading Fluency

-s	Plural (e.g. apples)
-er	More than (adj.) (e.g., higher)

The remainder of this chapter focuses on spelling and how the reading skills discussed fit together to help the struggling reader use all five components of the reading process. The following section outlines the general sequence of expected spelling skills (prekindergarten through about fifth grade), which lead to necessary encoding skills for reading. For additional multisensory methods and strategies, review also the online and printed resources provided in the Resource Section.

The Decoding Spelling Continuum with Grade-Level Expectations

Pre-K to Kindergarten
The continuum beginning in pre-K to kindergarten is the readiness stage. This stage is characterized by various activities to promote phonemic awareness. Listening skills are usually developed through hearing stories at home and at school. Pretend reading and spelling emerge. Also writing progresses from scribbles or letter-like forms to actual letters. The following characteristics in these early scribbles can

be linked to activities that will stimulate students' awareness of sounds that make up words to help them develop letter-sound understandings, which provides a knowledge base for spelling and reading. Children may demonstrate the following characteristics:

- Letter groupings formed in word-like units, forming word patterns.
- Use of one-letter spelling: U (you) and R (are), as used in text messages.
- Use of three- and four-letter spellings: I WNT HM (I want him).
- Phonetic spelling largely based on consonants: Mm CM HM (Mom come home).
- Expansion of phonetic spelling to include some consonants and vowels: H-P-V-A-L-N-T-N (happy valentine).

Some examples of activities in kindergarten may include (a) counting number of syllables in words, (b) listening and identifying a particular sound at the beginning, in the middle, and at the end of a word, and (c) counting a number of sounds in words by saying the sounds slowly and moving a pointer for each sound. By the end of prekindergarten, students should be fluent in naming the letters of the alphabet when pointed to on a chart and should be able to give the frequent, common sounds of consonants (e.g., *b, c,* and *f*) and short vowel sounds for *a, e, i, o, u,* as seen in Exhibit 6.8: Sample Words with Short Vowel Sounds.

Kindergarteners should be able to blend consonant sounds with short vowel sounds and create and read simple sentences (e.g., cat sat on the mat). They should also be able to rhyme words with the same vowel sound and same ending, sometimes referred to as rime (e.g., cup, up, sup, pup).

First Grade: The Decoding Spelling Continuum

First-graders are expected to know how to use both consonants and short vowel patterns to read and write simple sentences. Other patterns and rules to teach include: (a) When the long vowel sound is in the initial (beginning) or medial (middle) position and is followed by one consonant sound, *e* is added to the end of the word (e.g., name, same, five, rope, cube); (b) The "floss rule" helps student remember that after a short vowel, a final *f* is spelled *ff*, a final *l* is spelled *ll*, a final *s* is spelled *ss*, and a final *z* is spelled *zz* (e.g., tell, puff, class, buzz). Later, some exceptions should be taught, such as this, us, thus, yes, bus, quiz, and his.

Anglo-Saxon words with common consonants and vowel-sound-letter correspondences are taught in first grade. Students master the spelling of one-syllable words with one-to-one correspondences, such as the short vowels in words learned in kindergarten and the consonant sounds *b, d, f, g, h, l, m, n, p, s,* and *t*. They also learn a few common patterns from sounds that have more than one spelling, such as the *k* before *a, o, u,* or any consonant with *c* (e.g., cap, cot, cub, class, club). Before *e, i,* or *y,* the *c* sound is spelled with a *k* as in keep, kid, and skit.

Second Grade: Alphabetic Principles

By second grade the emphasis should be in guiding students to begin to understand rules of phonics, including consonants, short vowels, and word families. The first one hundred sight words (Anglo-Saxon words) should be introduced (see lists in Resource Section). Students are probably ready for more complex Anglo-Saxon letter patterns and common inflectional endings. It is a best practice to use letter patterns in one-syllable and two-syllable words.

The following spelling patterns are emphasized:

1. Final *k* sound after a short vowel in a one-syllable word is spelled *ck* (e.g., back, pack, sick, stick, sock). Final *k* sound after consonant or two vowels is spelled *k* (e.g., milk, desk, cook). Final *ch* sound after a short vowel in a one-syllable word is spelled *tch* (e.g., pitch, fetch, catch). After a consonant or two vowels, *ch* sound is spelled *ch* (e.g., couch, ranch). Exceptions are which, rich, much, and such.
2. Final *j* sound after short vowel in a one-syllable word is spelled *dge* and *ge* after a long vowel, a consonant, or two vowels (e.g., badge, bridge, age, strange, scrooge). Initial and medial *au* sound is usually spelled *ou*, and final *au* sound is spelled *ow* (e.g., out, found, bow, wow).

Second-graders also learn to spell words with inflectional endings, such as *ing* and *ed*. Words with these endings may require doubling or dropping a letter. For instance, when a suffix that begins with a vowel is added to a one-syllable word that ends in one vowel and one consonant, the final consonant is doubled (e.g., hopping, stopping, chopped, slapped). Likewise, when a suffix that begins with a vowel is added to the last syllable of a multisyllabic word that ends in one vowel and one consonant, it is stressed (e.g., beginning, occurred). When a suffix that begins with a vowel is added to a word that ends in a final *e*, the final *e* is dropped (e.g., staring, caring, sharing, poked, hoped).

Third Grade: Spelling Rules

Third-graders are ready to learn how to pronounce and spell multisyllabic words and the unstressed vowel *schwa*, as heard in about, afar, amount. The list of compound words should be expanded to include more words with simple (Anglo-Saxon) prefixes and suffixes (see list in the Resource Section). Students should be ready for more complicated syllable patterns including (a) *c* for the final *k* after a short vowel in words with more than one syllable (e.g., music, republic, picnic); (b) when *s* is a sound for *c* in the middle of a multisyllabic word after a vowel and when the *c* comes before *e, I,* or *y* (e.g., receive, icicle, cyclone); and (c) *k* says *k* and *ck* says *k* when they are at the end of a word or syllable directly after a single short vowel (e.g., clock, lock, deck); use *k* after a consonant, after a long-vowel sound and after two vowels (e.g., bank, cake, look).

Best instructional practices include the review of syllable patterns and segmenting syllables with clapping. Instruction may also involve guiding students in revisiting spelling rules for *j*, spelled *ge* and *dge*: use *dge* at the end of a word or syllable after a single short vowel (e.g., badge, dodge, smudge); use *ge* after a consonant, after a long-vowel sound, and after two vowels (e.g., hinge, page, fringe).

Students should also learn to spell words with common suffixes. A suffix (originating from Latin, Anglo Saxon, French, or Greek) is an ending added to a word to change its meaning. It may require changing a letter such as the following: change *y to i* when a suffix does not begin with *i* is added to a word that ends in a consonant and a final *y* (e.g., beautiful, happiness, pennies). Experts in spelling strategies recommend that the following suffixes are added to previous understandings by the end of third grade so that the students will be ready for the Doubling Rule: *-ed, -ing, -y, -er, -en, -est, -ish, -able, -ful, -ly, -less, -ness, -ment* (Rudginsky and Haskell 1985, 30).

Fourth Grade: Spelling Rules

It is hoped that fourth-graders are no longer in the process of learning to read and spell but are now *reading to learn*. They should be introduced to the Latin origin of words (prefixes, roots, and suffixes) and learn how to apply word patterns from Latin and Anglo-Saxon origins. On this level, there are additional rules of spelling, which may not have been mastered even though they were introduced earlier. Some of these rules are: the *ou* sound can be spelled *ou* or *ow*; use *ou* at the beginning or in the middle of a word (e.g., our, ought, around); when the *ou* sound is followed by a single *n, l, er,* or *el,* use *ow* (e.g., down, growl, flower, towel); *use ow* at the end of a word rather than *ou* (e.g., cow, how, now, allow); exceptions are powder, chowder, crowd, coward, and foul.

Key spelling rules have been included here, but space will not allow all spelling rules to be covered for all targeted grades from K–5. Although syllables are introduced in late kindergarten and first grade, the seven types of syllables are not recommended until around fourth grade and beyond. All lessons depend on the readiness level of the students, but the following seven kinds of syllables should be taught, in part, and reviewed from first through twelfth grades:

1. **Closed Syllable**
   a. The closed syllable ends with a consonant (cat, cat-e-go-ry).
   b. A single vowel before the final consonant in one-syllable words has a short sound (that, shot).
2. **Open Syllable**
   a. An open syllable ends with a vowel (e.g., fo-cus, du-ty).
   b. The vowel that has a long sound says its own name.
   e. An open syllable can be just one letter if that letter is a vowel (*a, I,* o-pen).
3. **VCE (vowel-consonant-e) Syllable or Magic E**
   a. The final *e* is silent in a vowel-consonant *e* syllable.
   b. The silent *e* at the end of the word makes the vowel before it have a long sound (cape, name, stripe).
4. **Vowel Team (grades three and up)**
   a. A vowel team usually has two vowels together that have one sound (e.g., *ea* in leaflet; *ee* in seaweed; *ai* in sailboat, *ay* in playtime, *oa* in oatmeal; *oe* in tiptoe).
   b. Be sure to notice whether a vowel combination is reversed (e.g., *oi* instead of *io* as in vi/o/lin). If the two vowels are reversed, divide between them.
5. **r-Combination Syllable (*r-controlled*) (grades three and up)**
   An *r*-combination syllable always has at least one vowel followed by *r*. The *r* always comes directly after the vowel (*ar, er, ir, or, ur,* and *ear*). The *r* gives the vowel a unique sound.
   a. The *s*tudent has already learned the sounds th*ese r*-combinations make (*s*tart, b*ir*d, burn/ing, learn, port, doc/tor, beg/gar, work).
6. **Consonant-le Syllable (c-le) (grades four and up)**
   a. A consonant-*le* syllable comes at the end of a word (cra/dle, bub/ble, ti/tle).
   b. A consonant-*le* syllable has no vowel sound. The silent *e* at the end of the syllable is the only vowel. Only the consonant and the *l* are pronounced.
7. **Diphthong Syllable (DT)**
   a. A diphthong syllable usually has two vowels together that have one sound (e.g., *ow* in prowler; *ou* in outline; *aw* in jigsaw; *au* in audit; *oi* in tinfoil; *oy* in enjoy; *oo* in cartoon, and *oo* in bookcase).
   b. The diphthong syllable has a special sound and may include letters that are not vowels or vowel substitutes such as *y* and *w* (sail, stay, snowing, light, eight).

Other than the common dictionary, it is difficult to find a source that teaches where to place an accent when there are two or more syllables in unfamiliar words.

The dictionary shows which syllable gets the stress—the one with the accent mark that looks like a little baseball bat—but does not state why. To create brain activity and memory, we recommend teachers have students *stamp* their feet when they read the syllable with the accent. In this way, students get a feel of the emphasis or accent. Rudginsky and Haskell (1985, 23–24) recommend three accent patterns to help determine which syllable gets the accent:

1. Accent the root of a word. We usually do not accent the prefix or suffix (e.g., con/duct', pro/ject', sub/mit', act'/ing).
2. If there are two syllables in a root, we usually accent the first syllable (e.g., tel'/e/gram, am'/ic/able).
3. In words of three or more syllables that end in a silent-*e* syllable, there is usually one syllable between the accented syllable and the silent-*e* syllable (e.g., ex/on'/er/ate ap/pro'/pri/ate, ac/cu'/mu/late, con/tam'/i/nate).

Fourth-graders should know the Y Rule. When adding suffixes to base words that end in *y*, the important process in this rule is whether a vowel or a consonant comes before the y. If a vowel comes before the *y*, keep the *y* and add any suffix. But, if a consonant comes before the y, change the *y* to *i* before adding a suffix *except* when the suffix begins with an *i*; then you keep the *y*. The following are among spelling rules for suffixes to be emphasized in the fourth-grade classroom. These rules and instructional information are adapted for teachers from a spelling text by Rudginsky and Haskell (1985).

Rule 1: If the letter before a final *y* is a vowel, the *y* doesn't change when you add a suffix (e.g., play, played, playful).

Exceptions to memorize: day + ly = daily, gay + ly = gaily; pay + ed = paid; say + ed = said; lay + ed = laid; mislay + ed = mislaid; slay + ed = slain.

Rule 2: If the letter before a final *y* is a consonant, the *y* changes to *i* when you add any suffix, except when the suffix begins with an *i*
(for example: carry, carried, carrying).

Exceptions to remember: shy + ly = shyly, dry + ness = dryness sly + ly = slyly; spry + ness = spryness. (All of these root words share the same suffix endings.)

Fifth Grade and Above

Fifth-graders should review previous rules of spelling especially in connection with vocabulary words drawn from literature and text read across the curriculum. Students should be introduced to common words with Greek origins. They should be able to identify word patterns from Latin, Anglo-Saxon, and Greek origins by first memorizing basic common affixes (prefixes and suffixes) and applying the understanding. For example, a *cloze* activity can be used: provide a sentence with an unfamiliar word that has to be deciphered based on meaning drawn from the word origin and context such as *protagonist*.

Other rules that may help students develop vocabulary while enhancing spelling skills are understanding the parts of speech of certain word endings and learning how to recognize these words in context. Students should know that *-us* and *-ous* sound alike and know how to use them in context. For example, *-us* is usually a noun ending (sinus, octopus), and *-ous* is always an adjective suffix. It is sometimes added to a noun to create an adjective (dangerous, miraculous). An exception is the word *celsius*, an adjective describing temperature.

Also some teachers review the Doubling Rule, the Silent-e Rule, and the Y Rule with students in fourth and fifth grades by assigning a rules poster (see Exhibit 6.8 for them to review at home and in study areas).

For students who consistently demonstrate difficulty with these skills, teachers should assess and identify the learning difficulty and plan immediately the necessary remediation and interventions. Learning these spelling rules, reading, and applying key words daily will provide the foundation needed for present and later reading and spelling success. Students should keep a spelling/reading notebook where learned words are used in dictated sentences.

Exhibit 6.8: The Doubling Rule

Double: Double the final consonant if the suffix begins with a vowel, but *do not* double when suffix begins with a consonant. (Example: sad + *er* = sadder; with a consonant, sad + *ness* = sadness).

Drop: Drop the final *e* if the suffix begins with a vowel. Keep the *e* if the suffix begins with a consonant (e.g., name, naming, nameless).

Change: Change the *y* to *I* if there is a consonant before the *y*. (e.g., cry, cried); however, *y* + *ing* are married and will never be separated (e.g., crying and staying). Keep the *y* if a vowel comes before the *y*, then add suffix (e.g., play + *ed* = played).

Source: Adapted from Rundinsky and Haskell 1985, 86.

Traditional Best Practices: Revisited

Educational research and history have determined that teachers, not programs, make the critical difference in whether students achieve and succeed in reading. Direct instruction is a highly structured teaching approach that is designed to accelerate the learning rate of at-risk students. Curriculum materials and instructional sequences attempt to move students to mastery at the fastest possible pace. During her first year of teaching, one of the authors was a student of Siegfried Engelmann who initiated the original program known as Distar (N-3). It was researched and developed during the late 1960s as part of Project Follow Through—a massive educational initiative of President Johnson's War on Poverty. Distar is better known today as one of the programs produced by the Science Research Associates (SRA) of Chicago, Illinois. The SRA Reading Laboratory is known also for producing leveled packets of reading intervention cards (grades one through twelve) that contain stories with self-checking activities in comprehension, vocabulary, and word-attack exercises to help struggling readers. This program is still one of the most effective classroom sets of materials designed to engage students of various reading abilities while addressing an identified reading skill.

One tool used in best practices is the flip folder that can be adapted to almost any subject area (see Exhibit 6.9). To illustrate this tool for a spelling assignment, cut one side of a manila file folder into thirds lengthwise to obtain three equal "flaps." Each flap should remain connected to the folder at the fold. On the first outer flap, list vertically "LOOK-ECHO-COVER"; in the center section, print "COPY, REVIEW, SAY"; and on the third flap, print "REWRITE." Insert a clean writing sheet (lengthwise) with three columns to align with the three, labeled sections. For accuracy, issue students a printed copy of spelling words (seven to twenty, depending on age). Have students paste the list under the first flap of the flip folder. Ensure understanding of pronunciation by calling out words for students to echo (repeat). If words are only listed on the board, some students may have difficulty copying correctly. Therefore, a printed list of spelling words placed under the first flap will be helpful.

Exhibit 6.9: Look, Echo, Copy, Rewrite Spelling Strategy

(Center Flap)	(Outer cover)	(Third Flap)
COPY REVIEW SAY	LOOK ECHO COVER	REWRITE WORDS
(Place spelling list under this label inside of Flip Folder)	(Students copy and review words for accuracy. Study word patterns if any.)	(Students work in pairs to pretest. One calls the words while the other writes the words.)

Other best practices include word sorting (using word patterns) and word games, ranging from word play creating small words from one multisyllabic word to making lists of words with the same beginning or ending.

Spelling and reading are acquired reciprocal abilities. Reading is an ability that promotes confidence. It adds to a person's ability to think, learn, write, and imagine. Whenever the reading ability is manifested through quality work, it empowers one to learn more. Learning more through reading is a process that should never end during a lifetime. Readers read to become proficient, just like an athlete practices to become great!

Traditional best practices are reflective of the needs of learners based on the research on student learning and schooling. Studies of older students (CORE 2004) have revealed that many students still need decoding and spelling skills taught until about eighth grade. Knowledge of morphemes (the smallest units of meaning in language) provides additional information to understand the following about words:

- The addition of the letter *s* to nouns makes them plural.
- Prefixes and suffixes provide additional meaning such as *re* meaning "back" or "again," unless it is in a word like *record* (a kept document).
- Greek and Latin roots are found within multisyllabic words and make up 60 percent of the English language.

The research in CORE (2001) has supported the premise that students need to encounter a spelling word about twelve times before they know it well enough to use it effectively as a part of their oral and written vocabulary. Other studies have indicated that profoundly dyslexic students can require as many as one hundred or more repetitions before the brain adapts to assimilate the new word (change made in the brain). To train teachers to accommodate the various learning styles and needs of student, educators have to truly "shake up the schoolhouse" and "invent better schools" (Schlechty 1997).

Reforming schools and school reform are terms traditionally used to describe the process by which schools are restructured and refocused to better serve the learning needs of students. Educators are beginning to realize that knowing the English language and knowing basic math skills will not provide a balanced education in a global market place. A blended education is being proposed to foster more meaningful and engaging student-centered instruction for all kinds of learners. Elementary schools need to address the needs of the whole child as ASCD (Association of Supervision and Curriculum Development) has proposed for several years. Young students need to learn how to balance understandings across content areas and apply grade-level problem-solving skills upon demand. Students should have practice in developing and using critical thinking skills to adapt and survive through the challenges of life involving social, educational, and economic pressures.

Secondary and older students, especially, need *blended learning* as explained by Cynthia Welmer who was cited in Laura Varlas's article in *Education Update* (ASCD, August 2011). Today's students need to understand by design as well as design and adapt their understandings. Students are under pressure to compete on the social network—trying be all things to scores of people. This is difficult. Many times youngsters lose personal identity and neglect to perfect personal talents and focus on career goals. Therefore, it is not just about school reform; it is more like school evolution. Schools have evolved to Dewey days of "learning by doing." Yet, in a technological age within a global society, universal common-core standards are needed for broader understanding.

Summary of Chapter Points

- The skills of reading, writing, and spelling are interrelated.
- Phonemic awareness is directly associated with learning to spell.
- Reading is both a tool and a skill that involves several components.

Teaching Tips

1. Demonstrate what good readers do: (a) select an interesting book, (b) allow students to discuss what they already know about the book, and (c) discuss what the author's purpose might be. Use read aloud method to share the book with the whole class, or in small groups.
2. While reading, (a). have students imagine things, and relate these incidents to their own lives, (b) create questions, and have students respond either verbally, or in writing to these questions.
3. After completing 1 and 2 above, work with students to clarify words, and ideas encountered: (a) allow students to share their ideas about the book, and (b) ask students if reading the book caused them to change their opinion about the topic.

Suggested Websites

Big IQ Kids: www.bigiqkids.com. Provides daily lessons to help students score 100 percent on every spelling and vocabulary test (use code: 103).

Bright Solutions for Dyslexia: www.dys-add.com. Provides readings, videos and other solutions for dyslexic students.

Institute for Multi-Sensory Education (IMSE): www.orton-gillingham.com. IMSE is committed to providing multisensory instruction of the highest quality, through direct and personal training, dramatically increasing the literacy skills of our children.

Intervention Central (IC): www.interventioncentral.org. IC provides free intervention and assessment resources for educators in grades K–12.

Suggested Readings/Resources

Dean, C. B., B. Stone, E. Hubbell, and H. Pitlet. 2012. *Classroom instruction that works: Research-based strategies for increasing student achievement.* 2nd ed. Alexandria, VA: ASCD.

Dougherty, E. 2012. *Assignment matter: Making the connections that help students meet standards.* Alexandria, VA: ASCD.

Eide, D. 2011. *Uncovering the logic of English: A common-sense solution to America's literacy crises.* Minneapolis, MN: Pedia Learning.

Fisher, D., and N. Frey. 2010. *Guided instruction: How to develop confident and successful learners.* Alexandria, VA: ASCD.

Hurford, D. M. 1998. *To read or not to read.* New York: A Lisa Drew Book/Scribner.

Reeves, A. R. 2011. *Where great teaching begins, planning for student thinking and learning.* Alexander, VA: ASCD.

Tyner, B. 2004. *Small-group reading instruction, A differentiated teaching model for beginning and struggling readers.* Newark, DE: International Reading Association.

UIS-AIMS and Literacy Assessment. n.d. Retrieved January 8, 2012, from www.unescobkk.org/education/planning-and-managing-education/aims/uis-aims-activities/uis-aims-and-literacy-assessment.

CHAPTER 7
Accountability and Support for Different Learners

Chapter Subheadings
Accountability of School Administrators
Accountability of Teachers
Instructional Accountability: A-to-Z Teaching Strategies
Accountability and Classroom Paraprofessionals
Classroom Management and Accountability

OBJECTIVES

- To address how school personnel can demonstrate accountability and support for diverse learners.
- To provide teaching strategies to meet the needs of all students, including the struggling unsuccessful student.

Terms to Know

Accountability: demonstration of concerted efforts to teach all students including the unsuccessful student.

Classroom Management: use of common procedures among school personnel to improve students' self-discipline and promote a disciplined learning environment.

Leadership: nurturing and supportive actions that result in collaboration and teamwork within the school.

After understanding the dyslexic student and the learning process, teachers must be accountable for all students under their tutelage. Teaching is a tremendous undertaking. It is not just an occupation; it is a *calling*. The best and most effective teachers feel the gut urge to make a difference in the lives of children. However, can all teachers be accountable for all areas of student learning from diverse populations? This chapter addresses this question and offers twenty-six teaching styles that may be effective in the process of teaching different learners. First, let's consider the educational accountability that is expected from administrators and teachers.

Accountability of School Administrators

School personnel are no longer the lone authority controlling and directing decisions such as retention and program activities of students. Rather, they are perceived as professional coworkers who, through their leadership in the decision-making process, collaborate with teachers, parents, and other community stakeholders to make decisions about student learning. School administrators are in a position to facilitate the dynamic, interactive process and ensure that all students are provided a school environment that promotes learning. All students should be stimulated and encouraged through differentiated instructional techniques to reach their maximum potential.

However, the students must also buy into the process. Discipline issues and disorderly conduct in the upper grades often emerge from deficient literacy skills. Teamwork and collaboration among school administrators are needed at the local, district, and state levels to address underlining student difficulties that may interfere with learning. Struggling readers need support from the administration, teachers, and parents in order to catch up and keep up. School administrators are expected to provide uniform procedures for identifying, diagnosing, and instructing all students and struggling readers. Teachers should then be given time to assess the students with necessary resources to provide the appropriate interventions. Too often, teachers report that there are *limited* resources and an *unlimited* number of learning differences among students. With diverse academic needs, there should be an action plan, which includes community stakeholders (parents, churches, clubs, and community centers), to address the needs of the school's demographic and to assist teachers as well as to hold them accountable.

Accountability of Teachers

Accountability is a word in the educational process that was widely studied and processed during the early to mid-2000s beginning with the No Child Left Behind mandate of 2001. Teachers could no longer pass students to the next grade without written evidence that concerted efforts had been made to teach the unsuccessful student. Standardized testing became the buzzwords that required schools to pretest and posttest students to determine the yearly progress made in that school year in a given subject. It was the general consensus that whatever went on in the classroom was the key to increasing student achievement. Accountability was expected throughout the school, ranging from the school climate to the building layout itself to the level of quality instruction. Instructional accountability ranged from the librarian and other paraprofessionals to the classroom teachers.

The historic Association for Supervision and Curriculum Development (ASCD) designed one of the most respected standards-based evaluation tools utilized nationally. The tool used observation and other tools to evaluate teachers based on their planning and preparation, classroom environment, instruction, and completion of professional development responsibilities. In addition to the ASCD's observation system, which balanced successful classroom instruction with output (student performance), there was a pre- and postcomparison to determine the areas of strengths and weaknesses.

If student behavior interfered with the learning process within the classroom the principal/school leader had to make sure that professional development for the teacher was made available.

As in other professions, teachers were expected to advance in their careers based on the quality of their work. Accountable teachers who demonstrated quality instruction were eligible for merit pay or compensated with incentives. On this point, many educational administrators feel that teacher compensation should not be tied only to the number of years served, graduate credits, and/or degrees earned. Members of the American Federation of Teachers have voiced the opinion that people from unrelated educational fields should not be allowed to teach without proper preparation; however, most teachers and administrators can name persons who entered the education arena through an alternate route and successfully adapted, contributing innovative strategies and skills that were effective in the classroom. But teachers and administrators can also list several who came into the profession who did not serve the students well, and students suffered at their hands.

For all dedicated and talented teachers who demonstrate an understanding of students and who almost naturally translate knowledge into bite-sized pieces so that learning can take place among all kinds of learners, we salute you. However, to assist with the many responsibilities that teachers have, A-to-Z quick tips have been provided in this chapter to help teachers, parents, and paraprofessionals match their teaching styles with the different learning styles.

Instructional Accountability: A-to-Z Teaching Styles and Strategies for Different Learners

A. Accentuate the positive: Accentuating the positive increases the dyslexic student's motivation. Dyslexic students learn differently. If a student completes an assignment but not as instructed, be sure to accentuate positively the correct parts first: "You certainly have made a great start, but I am sure you want to include—" This will help stimulate the student in a constructive way. Reviewing the requirements in a positive way will provide corrective instruction without frustration.

B. Be understanding: Understanding your students' needs is important. Many times the dyslexic student may appear unmotivated or slow. Due to lack of understanding these misconceptions can lead to frustration and low self-esteem. If the educator understands the learning process in the dyslexic person, this can help the student's self-esteem by knowing that the teacher understands her/his particular circumstances.

C. Communicate with your students: Communication leads to academic improvement. Arrange frequent meetings with your students. Talk about their improvement and where they may need improvement. Ask your students what learning techniques may work best for them. Follow up with a Learning Styles Survey as described in chapter 4. Communicating with your students helps them feel self-confident because they know what is going to happen next.

D. Develop a plan: Developing an action plan can help students set goals. Sitting down with your students and developing a plan will help students achieve their goals. Helping your students achieve their goals will help them to also realize their capabilities and increase motivation for learning. If the educator understands the dyslexic student and incorporates these tips, one can expect a more positive attitude and a higher level of achievement.

E. Encourage: Encourage your student. Having a learning disability can be a frustrating process. When improvements are made or something has been completed in a timely manner, remember a little encouragement can go a long way. For example, "Great job, I think you've got it!"

F. Follow up: Follow a scheduled time with students so you can evaluate their progress. During this time, allow students to express concerns about learning and classroom work. Make sure they conduct a self- evaluation. This will enable them to understand and analyze their own learning process.

G. Goals: Goal setting can be class goals or students can set personal goals. Once the goals are set give students a time frame. Once the goals are met, meet with students periodically and discuss their progress. This will help students value the development of planning, goal setting, and organization. Set both short-term and long-term goals.

H. Homework: Do your homework and make it easy for dyslexic students to complete theirs. Dyslexia is a learning difference. Don't be discouraged if you don't see progress immediately. Organize. Have colored containers for homework assignments and for completed homework. Short on time? Permit homework sheets to be issued per week, or have quick students to be responsible for making a copy from the board for the ones who struggle.

I. Intelligence: Intelligence comes in different colors, sizes, and shapes. Emphasize the strong points of particular types of intelligences and learning styles within diverse cultures. For example, differentiate instruction by allowing students to complete projects geared toward their "intelligence." Researching and becoming an expert at something usually boosts self-esteem.

J. Journal: Journaling can help everyone. Acquire notebooks or journals to demonstrate the reflective benefits of journaling. After students appreciate and understand the process, ask students to write about their goals, accomplishments, fears, etc. Teach them that their journal is their safe place to express themselves without fear, judgment, or ridicule. This will improve their writing and creativity. (Caution them about sharing personal or family matters that should be private.)

K. Knowledge: Knowledge never ends. Encourage students to think outside the box. Tell them that knowledge and learning never end. Reading is the best way to increase knowledge. Therefore, have a variety of books available for browsing and leveled reading.

L. Love: Teach students to love themselves, and know that they are loved. At a young age children begin to judge themselves by their personal appearance, grades, and friends. Encourage the development of character, interests, and talents. Students should know that it is important to do their best but at the same time, a letter grade does not define a person's worth. Encourage parents to teach this at home as well. (A–L code words were adapted from online information shared by International Dyslexia Association at www.IDA.org.)

M. Monitor: Monitor the progress of struggling learners. Use research-based interventions for each identified need, and keep a dated record of the response to interventions. Identify concepts or skills that were taught to accommodate the students' needs.

N. No child should be left behind: No child should be embarrassed for making mistakes, or for not learning at the expected grade level. Students with learning differences may also have behavioral issues. Solicit help from the teacher-support team and principal. Teachers may also want to set aside instructional time when the student(s) can be included in a small group and establish a sense of belonging.

O. Orton-Gillingham: Orton-Gillingham is the hyphenated name of Dr. Samuel T. Orton, neurologist, and Anna Gillingham, educator, at the New York Neurological Institute. They are the originators of the multisensory therapy and research-based method of direct instruction designed to accommodate learning-different children beginning in the primary grades through secondary school where older students have been identified with profound characteristics of dyslexia.

P. Plan lessons: Plan lessons that are strategic and sequential—building on previous lessons. Lessons should appeal to at least three of the five senses for most tactile learners to absorb and maintain the information given. For the visual learners, an example or a demonstration of what is expected will be effective.

Q. Quitting: Quitting is not an option for the struggling student, parent, or teacher of the struggling student. Sometimes the learning style can be confusing and frustrating to the student personally. The student needs encouragement and academic support. Refrain from using labels like "lazy and dumb." Use the hands-on strategies outlined in chapters 4 and 5 as well as those in the Resource Section.

R. Research: Research about the brain is increasing and there is more help for the dyslexic student. "With the right kind of intensive instruction, the brain can begin to permanently rewire itself and overcome reading deficits, even if it can't entirely eliminate them" (Carnegie Mellon University 2008, pp. 1-2). Remedial Instruction Can Make Strong Readers Out of Poor Readers, Brain Imaging Study Reveals. *ScienceDaily*, Retrieved from www.scieencedaily.com/releases/2008/06/080611103900.htm.

S. SchwabLearning.org: SchwabLearning.org is a wonderful website created by the Charles and Helen Schwab Foundation. Charles Schwab, a financial genius, is dyslexic and, therefore, established a foundation to support parents and teachers of children with this learning difference. Famous dyslexic adults like Henry Winkler share testimonies of their struggles in school and their victory in coping with this "lifelong companion" by focusing on their strengths.

T. Testing: Testing for dyslexia is not as simple as pretesting for general knowledge. Dyslexia is an inherited neurological language disability that affects the way one perceives print, responds to print in writing, spelling or reading. The "fingerprint" of the left brain determines whether the learning difference will be mild or profound in one or all of these language/reading areas. Generally, six or more tests are used to determine the exact areas of need and where immediate interventions should be focused. (See the Resource Section for lists of recommended tests that should be administered by a certified or professionally trained administrator.)

U. Uniqueness: Uniqueness is the best description of the brain. United efforts must be fostered among parents, teachers, and administrators to ensure that proper interventions are used to meet the needs of struggling different learners. Many will suffer through classes trying to memorize all the information. Some will begin to act out in class, taking away quality time from their peers as well as the focused attention of the teacher. All students were not recorded as students with disabilities, but most had reading difficulties that placed them about two years below grade level. Jannie Johnson, preventive counselor, found in her thirty years of working with troubled youth that when "unique" students find a good reason to discontinue unwanted behavior, their grades improve.

V. Virtual: Virtual learning is a great support for different learners. Technology and brain research have made immense strides in making tasks like test taking and note taking much easier for the different learner. *Ghotit Dyslexia Assistive Technology* networks with many schools at little or no cost. (Get more details online at www.ghotit.com.)

W. Writing: Writing is sometimes the only area that suffers among those with dyslexic tendencies. This deficiency is referred to as dysgraphia. People or students with dysgraphia should be taught forming letters by first seeing the letters demonstrated on large paper or white board with colored markers. The Texas Scottish Rite Dyslexia Training Program has students to first sky write the letters before attempting to write on paper. Individual lessons build on the previous lesson until automaticity and application are developed. Writing assignments should be preceded by meaningful discussions with visuals and other multisensory engagement before independent writing of ideas.

X. The *x*: This sound is a difficult sound for dyslexics to master. Therefore, a phonics program could be placed in the listening center supported by one-on-one modeling of the sound. Find words that have the letter in the beginning, middle, and end of words. Repetition of the sound in different locations makes a difference in the depth of understanding (e.g., xylophone, box, X-ray).

Y. You are important: *You* and *u* are difficult for struggling readers. One student wondered how the *u* can be pronounced *u* and the word *you* can also be pronounced *u*. We recommend that teachers discuss meaning: one is a person, and the other is a letter. General homonyms can also be taught with meaningful demonstrations using objects, scenarios, and role playing.

Z. Zealously zipping through lessons: Zipping through lessons is not the best practice for struggling readers. Lessons should be strategic, direct, and systematic. Carefully designed reviews at the end of lessons and at the beginning of new lessons help students with retention of information. There should be strategic connection with prior knowledge before concepts can be mastered and before new learning can become a part of long-term memory.

These twenty-six strategies and support statements are provided to help teachers accommodate students that may appear in the classroom with learning differences. Most teachers try to be fair in the classroom because that is generally the democratic way. However, sometimes teachers have to be equitable, that is, do what is equal under the circumstances but not addressed the same way.

School administrators can help close the achievement gap by engaging teachers and students in authentic pedagogy (Schlecthy 1997; Shaywitz 2004) using multidimensional leadership to see that things get done. Schools sometimes have strong leaders who are weak managers and vice versa (Cunningham and Cordeiro 2000). However, the best administrators are good at both leadership and management (Fullan 1999). These virtues may be difficult to acquire, but they are required for leadership effectiveness (Graseck 2005). School administrators should demonstrate leadership that is nurturing, supportive, and value endowed in order to create learning communities to enhance literacy. School administrators are expected to provide quality leadership that directs the path for school wide success. They are professionals who, though still central in the decision-making process, should collaborate with teachers to make decisions while remaining accountable for the effective leadership and management of the educational organization.

Accountability and Classroom Paraprofessionals

Over the years, we have seen how assistant teachers in the early grades complemented the learning environment in ways that allowed the teacher to concentrate on overall planning and integrating whole-group instruction with small groups and cooperative group activities. In the whole group, students were introduced, for example, to the concepts and goals for the day, providing content, demonstrations, and discussions so that students could relate to the subject. Segments were discussed in steps and procedures. The small groups or centers were then arranged so that the assistant teacher (or aide) would be responsible for certain groups, many times the blue group because they had the "blues."

However, over time, budget restraints required that the assistants would no longer have one class but several to which to report. Stability and systematic instruction were no longer available in the learning environment. This fact alone, along with limited resources and lack of student readiness for learning, influenced the dismal outcome of test scores and general student achievement.

Technology is probably the savior for what ails classrooms today. Many school systems will not have the finances to purchase computers with updated software, individual iPods, and electronic notebooks to truly individualize instruction. However, the investment for equipment and training would be far less than the traditional paraprofessionals who helped students in small groups with lessons for that day.

Classroom Management and Accountability

To improve self-discipline of students and prevent students from dropping out because of their deficient literacy skills, teamwork and collaboration are needed at the local, district, and state levels. To catch up and keep up, struggling readers need support from the administration, teachers, parents, and community stakeholders. The administrators and teachers must have common procedures for identifying, diagnosing, and instructing struggling readers. Teachers must be given time to assess the students with resources to provide the necessary interventions. The interventions used must be research based with considerations for influences, such as poverty.

In addition to environmental effects, a student may also have profound characteristics of dyslexia. That means he or she may have deficiencies in one area of reading, or may have weaknesses in several. This could be the reason many writers refer to these diverse readers as *struggling readers* because several dyslexic tendencies may be exhibited are found among other learning styles and different environmental conditions.

The effect of disruptive behavior on learning can be a factor. To curtail dropouts, discipline issues and disorderly conduct in the upper grades that often emerge from deficient literate skills must be addressed. All school personnel should have common procedures for identifying, diagnosing, and instructing struggling readers that may lead to curtailing disruptive behavior and dropouts. Time to assess students and the availability of necessary resources to provide the appropriate interventions are crucial in the management process.

Classroom management and accountability for student learning are influenced by many factors. If classroom teachers could engage students of all ages in ways that made social and realistic sense, more learning would likely take place. Under President Barack Obama's administration, much attention was given to creating jobs because the country had not experienced financial crises of this magnitude since the Great Depression. Under the Bush administration, it was reported that dishonesty had emanated from Wall Street, oil giants, and large real-estate investment companies to mismanagement of investments of private citizens, causing loss of retirement pensions, housing problems, and layoffs. Students and parents were affected during these times of crises. Teachers, already overworked due to teacher shortages, were now being cut from the payroll. Now, the school as a whole experienced *disciplined learning*. All had to make tough choices.

However, for teenagers or young adults, these tough times could be even more difficult to accommodate. Sometimes a simple event like a favorite teacher being laid off could cause a disruption in learning due to the student's fragile self-confidence. Many students from diverse economic cultures lack social skills that are adequate to handle these tough times. Finances are limited, so choosing quick solutions become the common plan. Long-term consequences are ignored and education is no longer the priority for so many of these young people. Unfortunately, some think that establishing a "family on the street" will solve financial and social needs and will, therefore, yield to the culture of delinquency. Too many students drop out of high school and tell their families that they will get a GED later; however, 33 percent of school dropouts never return to complete their education.

Many of these dropouts can be found in the prison population. When the prison population was studied, about 70 percent of the inmates had reading difficulties (NICHD 2004). Reading is still the primary skill that everyone needs, even in tough economic times. Students from kindergarten through high school still need the positive guidance of the classroom teacher. To help more struggling readers move toward grade-level performance, teachers are still accountable for offering various ways to accomplish the same academic goal, and encourage students for each sincere effort made despite the economic or social climate.

The next chapter addresses school reform and school evolution as viewed from descriptive and action research. Attention is given to how some of the best practices of the past are still effective, but the approach is different. Technology plays a major role in how information is presented in the school evolution.

Summary of Chapter Points

- School personnel, parents, and the community are accountable for providing opportunities so that diverse learners can reach their maximum potential.
- Accountability can be expected in teaching all kinds of learners through these twenty-six or more strategies (A–Z), and others that are being discovered by innovative teachers, even today.

- Accountability in support of different learners is influenced by many factors including the economic and social environments.

Teaching Tips

1. Review teaching tips located within the Resource Section of the Appendices, choose a word-based information sheet that will help in preparation reading intervention lessons for struggling readers. Materials needed: Chart, paper, this textbook, story and resource books, markers, and posting tape.
2. Participants work in small groups to create one "working-with-words_ intervention activity for struggling readers. Select a recorder, and a speaker within each group. Be sure to describe the elements of the lesson (e.g. STUDENT LEARNING STYLES, READING LEVEL, LESSON PROCEDURE, CONTENT, EVALUATION, and FOLLOW-UP). Post the completed chart in a general area.
3. Each small group should be prepared to explain with the group, the focus of the lesson. At the end of the presentation, invite feedback from co-participants regarding the strong, and weak points. (Record feedback and, show appreciation of the constructive input) If desired, each group recorder could type, and email an edited copy to a designated person for distribution to the whole group.

Suggested Readings/Resources

Dougherty, E. 2012. *Assignment matter, making the connection that help students meet standards*. Alexandria, VA: ASCD.

Eide, D. 2011. *Uncovering the logic of English, a common-sense solution to America's literacy crisis*. Minneapolis, MN: Pedia Learning.

Moats, L. 2000. *Speech to print*. Baltimore, MD: Brookes Publishing.

Moats, L., and K. E. Dakin. 2008. *Basic facts about dyslexia & other reading problems*. Baltimore, MD: The International Dyslexia Association.

Tyner, B. 2004. *Small-group reading instruction, A differentiated teaching model for beginning and struggling readers*. Newark, DE: International Reading Association.

CHAPTER 8

School Reform and the Evolving Modern Classroom

Chapter Subheadings
School Reform: Where Do We Go from Here?
Literacy: The Root of Academic Success
Addressing Diversity in the Classroom
Literacy Strategies for Struggling Diverse Learners

OBJECTIVE
To provide awareness of school and classroom processes that facilitates literacy development.

Terms to Know
No Child Left Behind Act (2001): a reauthorization of the Elementary and Secondary Act of 1965 designed to close the achievement gap with accountability, flexibility, and choice, so that no child is left behind; act holds schools more accountable for students reaching the same state standards in reading and mathematics by 2014.

Benjamin Bloom's Taxonomy: a framework first published in 1956 that describes the levels of learning; a system that has been used for decades.

To promote effective school reform, school administrators must first develop a plan for a strategic alliance that creates conditions whereby purpose, values information, and relationships are meaningfully connected and aligned around the school system's desire to develop an integrated and technologically supported curriculum (Brulle, Graseck, and Goldberg 2005; McEwan 2003). There should clearly be a process in place to build on the capacity of everyone in the school to expand the school's collective intelligence (Cunningham 2000). This plan should examine a variety of ways to distribute power throughout the school (Senge 2002), encourage and manage input from diverse stakeholders, and define the different roles of the staff within the new organizational structure. The overall goal should be to create ways to empower the school's personnel throughout the school district to enhance their self-worth and earn greater respect for the school as a whole and for each person who is committed to making a difference in the lives of the students and families of the served community.

School Reform: Where Do We Go from Here?

The federal No Child Left Behind Act (2001) sets targets requiring every student to reach proficiency by 2014. Most states set their own proficiency standards based on national standards aligned with federal trajectory. Some states have been accused of having lower academic standards and easier tests and, therefore, appear to be doing very well. However, Mitchell Chester, education commissioner of Massachusetts with 937 elementary, middle, and high schools, is strongly opposed to making the state test easier in order to look good on a federal report card. Chester's leadership elevates Massachusetts students to the top of comparison charts on national and even international standardized tests. His philosophy of excellence is among those that should be emulated.

To promote school reform nationwide, the school administrator often must boldly lead by "shaking up the schoolhouse" (Schlechty 2000) to ensure the necessary reforms are made. The school administrators stress that the No Child Left Behind Mandate of 2002 reduced the autonomy of school leaders to lead the school in some traditional ways that were still effective. There are some facts regarding children who are, by public policy, left behind. In 2002, Thomas and Bainbridge reported that of the 10.5 million children whose parents were contacted regarding health issues, most lived in conditions of poverty that denied their children the opportunity to develop their full cognitive potential. The child poverty rate in the United States is among the highest in the developed nations. These children are often left behind before they even enter the school building. However, with the passing of the Health Care Reform Bill of 2010, no child should be left behind in terms of health care. No child should be at risk due to chronic illnesses and diseases. No child should be left behind because the teacher is inadequately prepared to teach in the way students learn. Additionally, no teacher should be left behind because the higher educational system did not prepare him or her for the multifaceted challenge of educating students for the twenty-first century.

From the federal standpoint, the Title I educational program is designed for improving the academic achievement of the disadvantaged. Part D of Title I has prevention and intervention programs for children and youth who are neglected, delinquent, or at-risk. The Title I law under the evolving No Child Left Behind Act is authorized to execute the law with threefold objectives designed to

1. improve educational services for neglected or delinquent children and youth in local and state institutions so that such children and youth have the opportunity to meet the same challenging state academic *content* and *achievement* standards that all other children in the state are expected to meet;
2. provide targeted children and youth with the services needed to make a successful transition from institutionalization to further schooling or employment; and
3. prevent at-risk youth (neglected, disadvantaged or delinquent) from dropping out of school, and provide a support system to ensure continued education for existing dropouts and for children and youth returning from correctional facilities or alternative educational institutions (NCLB 2004; USDE 1999, 2002).

Many experts contributed to the construction of the NCLB Act to ensure that all elements of the population were represented (National Reading Panel 1999; US Department of Education 1999, 2000). However, the two most reoccurring fallacies in the act are (a) the government underestimated the number of low-performing schools in the nation, and (b) numerous states need more funds than were budgeted to fully implement all the components of the NCLB. For example, expecting all schools to have their students literate by third grade is idealistic but unrealistic in many situations where diverse learning styles require diverse timetables. Also, qualified teachers are not always available to keep the younger students or advanced students progressing while providing interventions for those who have already been left behind. To add to the grim state of literacy, the National Institute of Child Health and Human Development (1999, 2000) reported that about 40 percent of the adult population cannot read technical materials or does not choose to read for pleasure. This isn't surprising given that families who live in poverty seldom subscribe to the local newspaper. Children do not see adults read on a regular basis unless they searching the classified ads for jobs or garage sales.

Schools have, for decades, looked to the policies and procedures of successful businesses through the eyes of mid-twentieth-century organizational experts like Peter Drucker. Historically, businesses were perceived as the blueprint for schools to pattern their organizational structure (Sergiovanni, Burlingame, Coombs, and Thurston 1999). In businesses and in schools, administrative organizational patterns have increasingly become similar (Lashway 1999). To outline the salient parallels of businesses and schools, researchers noted several key dimensions related to leadership and administration (Eiter 2002). These dimensions included the following: (a) the leader as a strategic thinker; (b) the leader as a force of change (Fullan 1999); (c) the leader as a facilitator (Webster 2000); (d) the leader as coach (McEwan 1998); (e) the leader as creator or champion of culture (Thomas and Davis 2000); (f) the leader as decision maker (Fullan 2000; Seyfarth 2002); and, lastly, (g) the leader as driver for results (McEwan 1998, 2003). School administrators need all of these social, academic, and leadership skills to reform and refine some aspects of the educational system while others should *evolve—move gradually from a primitive to a more organized modern status.*

Why say education *evolves*? Even though the process of education is constantly changing, there are principles and theories of learning that should remain, and they generally do. For example, the historic Benjamin Bloom's Taxonomy first published in 1956 describes the levels of learning that have been used for decades. More recently, the levels have been revisited by educators, including Tressa Decker and Kay Davidson in *Bloom's & Beyond*. In the book, the authors define each level, align them with Bloom's theory, and provide graduated activities with appropriate probing questions for grades K–6. Thus, the original principles are maintained in the more recent version.

Writing methods have also evolved. More than eight hundred graphic organizers have been used across content areas, ranging from the Venn diagram to what some referred to as spider maps until thinking maps were developed by Dr. David Hyerle in 1988. Those searching for ways to illustrate critical thinking in a consistent format were drawn to Hyerle's book *Thinking Maps*, published by Innovative Sciences. This book, along with *Write from the Beginning* and other related texts, became widespread during the 1990s. The maps outline fundamental thinking processes based on the theory that the brain perceives the environment in the various formats of circles and lines. Hyerle designed eight basic maps for all levels of critical thinking and to encompass all disciplines.

Though still evolving, the writing applications for academic subjects and the graphing of critical thinking have transformed the quality of writing in several school districts throughout the country, helping struggling writers to become more proficient writers. These enhancements to the old to form the new are refreshing and exciting. Each generation of educators and researchers should indeed duplicate and improve existing research in order to improve the present level of student achievement and to meet the global needs of the current school population.

Literacy: The Root of Academic Success

The general consensus of educational leaders is that literacy is a broad-ability skill that is critically needed by not only students but all humankind. Developmental literacy is the ability to decode and read print in a progressive intellectual manner to gain meaning, to communicate, and to solve problems. The United Nations Educational, Scientific and Cultural Organization defines literacy as the "ability to identify, understand, interpret, create, communicate, compute and use printed and written materials associated with varying contexts" (Yousif 2003; UNESCO Education Sector 2004).

Sometimes budgetary constraints limit how much schools can do, but these limitations should not dictate the creativity of teachers and school leaders. Struggling readers are students too, and school administrators must use all available resources necessary to ensure that all students learn to their maximum potential. It is critical for teachers to have the required educational resources and to become knowledgeable about implementation strategies that are aligned with common-core standards.

To support teachers and school administrators, ASCD has recently collaborated with McREL (an educational research and development corporation) to develop a common-core web page (see ASCD website) that goes beyond *Understanding Common Core State Standards* (John Kendall 2011) and tracks state standards adoption throughout the United States. ASCD will provide ongoing implementation resources that can be shared among states, districts, schools, and educators.

With limited budgets, schools can now reach beyond the central and state offices to broad online national and federal resources to find both economical and educational solutions. Currently, more than ever, school leaders are looking to local businesses, online businesses, philanthropic foundations, national television hosts, and even sports icons to acquire strategic support for their students.

To promote literacy across all age groups, Moats (1999) and other researchers (McEwan 2002; Miller 2002; Neuman and Dickinson 2001) recommend effective reading instruction for students with reading difficulties. Their recommendations can be summarized as providing

- direct teaching of decoding, comprehension, and literature appreciation;
- phoneme awareness instruction related to rich experiences and story text;
- systematic and explicit instruction in the code system of written English;
- daily exposure to a variety of texts, as well as incentives for children to read independently and with others;
- vocabulary instruction that includes a variety of complementary methods designed to explore the relationships among word usage, structure, origin, and meaning;

- comprehension strategies that include establishing prior knowledge, prediction of outcomes, summarizing, clarification, questioning, and visualization; and frequent reflective writing of prose to enable deeper understanding of what is read; employing opportunities to explore with metacognition (thinking about thinking) (McEwan 2004, 33–60).

Recent research concluded that children who are severely disadvantaged frequently have difficulty with cognitive development, especially school-readiness skills, adequate vocabulary, and other literacy skills required for learning to read effectively (Allington 2001; Lyons 2001; Routman 2002). Many of these children are left behind very early in the process, and the reform of NCLB did not adequately address those deficiencies (Brulle 2005).

So far, a review of relevant research-based literature on the accountability and perceptions of elementary-school administrators in the literacy instruction of struggling readers has been presented. Views were provided from both sides of the educational spectrum—those who perceive and readily accept the responsibility of accountability and those who challenge the accountability of political stakeholders who do not provide necessary financial resources. The four major challenges school administrators face are (1) ensuring that struggling readers and students achieve at their highest potential, (2) recruiting and maintaining qualified teachers, (3) providing proper resources, and (4) offering professional development so that best practices will be used to promote the development of a literate population and responsible productive citizens (Routman 2002; Schlechty 1997).

Various stakeholders often discuss the financial investment versus the accountability of school leaders and needed outcomes in addressing the issues of developing literacy. Illiteracy is the number-one problem in America (National Reading Panel 200X; NCLB 2000). McEwan (1998, 2002) and other experts (Fullan 1999; Portin 2004; Sergiovani 1999; Taylor 1947) propose some characteristics that are worthy of consideration in addressing literacy. Portin (2004), especially, stressed that administrators must first identify what schools need based on students' test scores and data compiled on student performance (Rothstein 2004). While test data are currently used more effectively to drive instruction since the NCLB of 2000, educators frequently complain that assessment data and the necessary resources to implement interventions are difficult to acquire. Budget cuts have caused educational organizations and educational leaders (Scherer 2004) to questions the constitutionality of No Child Left Behind (2000, 2001) since adequate funds were not legislated to finance the mandate (Lashway 1999; Anderson and Roit 2001; Camilli and Yureck 2001). Demands on school districts across the country are high, but budgets are low (Scherer 2004).

However, in this accountability era, everyone in education is expected to accept the challenge and provide leadership in improving a quality education for every child (Lyons and Shaywitz 2003; McEwan 1998). Scherer (2004), reporting from an interview with Rod Paige, former secretary of education, also stated that schools need to educate those who many call hard-to-teach or struggling learners. School administrators and teachers should conduct a needs assessment and share findings with colleagues. These identified needs should lead to a strategic plan whereby more time is spent exploring what students are learning and how administrators can effectively perform their jobs as instructional leaders (Routman 2002; Schlecthy 1997).

Paige also pointed out that school leaders who isolate themselves from their respective communities often create major problems (Scherer 2004) because community collaboration is an advantage (Schwahn and Spady 2001; Senge 1994, 2002). Schools need parents and community stakeholders to volunteer, to serve as judges for academic contests, and to participate in special events. Getting these significant others and stakeholders in the schools is like having a blowout sale at a department store. If a business can get customers in the door, it knows that someone will buy its products. Schools must take advantage of these vital human resources so these leaders will buy-in, reaching academic goals of schools in respective communities.

Addressing Diversity in the Classroom

Obviously, the diversity of students and the demographics of schools have changed and expanded over the last fifteen years. This has created a great challenge for teachers and administrators. Some characteristics of diversity among today's school population include not only the traditional racial mix, ethnicity, national origin, and culture but also diversity of age and native language. Also, diversity may be noticed in the behavior of disgruntled students who have been retained in a grade or from students bused in from other zones to create racial or socioeconomic balance or to justify having certain academic programs.

Student diversity is greater today than at any time in the history of America. As a consequence, as indicated here and by numerous educational researchers, literacy has ignited the attention of educators and politicians from the White House to the small rural school in the Deep South. Reading experts have been employed throughout the country to study reading instruction and provide research-based proposals to the National Reading Panel, of the US Department of Education, in order to establish common grounds for addressing literacy. These studies, mentioned throughout this book, have presented effective strategies and best practices that should be used in teaching reading.

To support students, teachers, and school administrators without extensive additional costs to the parents or the school district, the Texas Scottish Rite Hospital for Children in Dallas, Texas, has researched and provided resources over several decades for children and adults with dyslexia. One of several handouts available is an unpublished document entitled "Suggestions for Helping a Student with Dyslexia." This informational has been very helpful to teachers with inadequate training and to teachers who constantly seek more effective ways to accommodate different kinds of learners with similar needs.

The National Institute of Health (NIH) studies thousands of students and adults with reading deficiencies. These studies have discovered learning styles and learning differences that have modified instruction and the way educators have approached reading difficulties among struggling readers for more than two decades. For example, one NIH study, conducted over twenty years ago, found that the ratio of boys to girls with dyslexia was not 3 boys to 1 girl, but 1.2 boys to 1 girl (Hurford 1998). However, another study conducted by a British researcher (Rutter 2005), involving 10,000 subjects, found that the number of boys with characteristics of dyslexia was significantly higher than the number of girls. Similarly, one urban school district of 31,000 students documented over a five-year period the number of students referred to the District Support Team for diagnostic testing and reported that the percentage of boys was much higher than that of girls (Jackson Public Schools 2008). Since researchers seem to disagree on gender comparisons, this may be a subject that needs additional research.

In a descriptive research study, strategies and programs endorsed by the National Reading Panel were surveyed to determine how familiar the administrators and teachers were with these best practices and programs. More than 80 percent of the professionals appeared to be familiar with the strategies and programs. However, the high percentage of professional development and the degree of understanding of best practices that the professionals indicated did not alter their decision to often retain students in the same grade for an additional year or two. Rather than apply the best intervention practices learned, 49.1 percent in a random sample of four hundred teachers and administrators relied on *retention* (remaining in the same grade) as the *practiced* literacy intervention in this urban school study. Participants in the sample felt they could more easily justify retention rather than promotion.

Literacy Strategies for Struggling Diverse Learners

Learning Styles and the African American Student
This research is significant to the African American communities because some school districts have indicated that student data tend to show that predominately

African American males are referred for academic assistance at a higher rate than girls (Crockett, 2005). Educators have indicated that lack of focus or disruptive behavior often lead to low academic performance among these students. Nonetheless, according to Boykin (2002), there are at least nine dimensions to African American culture that could be tapped into to enhance learning situations:

1. Spirituality. The general belief that powers greater than humanity exist and are at work.
2. Harmony. The belief that people and their environment are interdependently connected. This applies to integrating the parts of one's life into a harmonious whole.
3. Movement. A rhythmic orientation to life that may be manifested in music and dance as well as in behavior and approach.
4. Verve. The psychological aspect of the movement dimension and involves a preference to be simultaneously attuned to several stimuli rather than a singular, routine, or bland orientation—energetic, intense.
5. Affect. Emotional expressiveness and sensitivity to emotional cues, integration of feelings with cognitive elements.
6. Communalism. Interdependence of people; social orientation.
7. Expressive individualism. A person's unique style or flavor in an activity and spontaneity, manifested in a unique tilt of a hat, a walk, or a jazz musician's rendition.
8. Orality. Coined word for a form of oratory that emphasizes the importance of information learned and transmitted orally (e.g., call and response pattern).
9. Social time perspective. Time is viewed in terms of the event rather than the clock. For example, an event begins when everyone arrives (Willis and Yuhas, 2002).

In a workshop conducted by Madge Gill Willis and Jan Yuhas (2002) entitled "Learning Styles of African American Children," they offered some sobering points about the learning styles of African Americans. Three points relative to African American learning styles were discussed: (1) underlying assumptions about black children's learning styles that may be inconsistent due to the wide range of value systems and/or educational preparation of parents; (2) characteristics of their learning styles that may be due to lack of educational exposure rather than a disability; and (3) general preference for teachers who are fair but firm, consistent, and caring.

One assumption is that a learning style is a way of perceiving, conceptualizing, and problem solving. The African American culture is often diversified through cognitive orientations, attitudes, behavior, and personality. *Caring*, for example, may be interpreted as being fair and demanding while insisting on quality academic work with reachable intrinsic and/or tangible rewards. In our experience, black students, both males and females, tend to appreciate fairness more than undeserved "leniency" due to, say, social, educational, and economic conditions.

Assessment Strategy
The "Checklist for Identifying Reading Styles and Related Behavioral Differences" was developed out of necessity to help teachers match targeted students' reading and learning styles. The survey form grew out of ten years of observing and reviewing hundreds of referrals and has become a reliable instrument for showing indicators of dyslexia. Once the parents are informed of their child's learning style (identified through the survey form), a conference is scheduled with teachers and counselors.

The survey instrument was tweaked over a five-year period: three major categories were delineated to detect and profile the characteristics of dyslexia among students in both elementary and secondary schools. Additionally, the instrument was cross-checked by teachers throughout an urban school district to determine if the learning-style items on the form matched the results of a professionally tested group of students

It was noted, however, that where there were weak signs of dyslexia or a lack of clear determination, the psychologists made the same or similar observations as the examiners who used the checklist form presented in chapter 4. No student's documented analyses were reviewed by the examiner of the survey form prior to completing the form with the student. Teachers or the examiner had to observe the student's learning behavior or work samples at least four weeks prior to assessing the student and recommending accommodations for the learning style.

Students who continue to struggle with reading and learning after grade three will likely continue the struggle throughout adulthood when literacy and productivity are required for success.

Strategies for Struggling Diverse Learners
After determining the learning style and weaknesses of the student, procedures for completing assignments should be presented in small sequences. Procedures include developing dictionary skills. One approach for teaching dictionary skills is to divide the dictionary into four equal parts, called quartiles. To help students remember the four parts, the following mnemonic device can be used: create a numbered list from one to four. On the left, next to the numbers, write the initials for "An Elephant Madly Stomps" (A, E, M, S), and on the right of those letters, place a dash and write the initials for "Dinosaurs Love Raw Zebras" (D, L, R, Z). It should look like this:

1. A–D
2. E–L
3. M–R
4. S–Z

After some practice with the quartiles, some teachers find a triad to be more balanced: A to E, F to Q, and R to Z. Teachers and students can create their own mnemonic device during their dictionary study.

During the dictionary word study, students also develop skill using guide letters in words as well as guide words on the dictionary pages. First, the teacher identifies the initial letter as the guide letter using word cards to be arranged in alphabetical order, as in seat, home, name, and so on. Then, the teacher gradually increases the difficulty by giving words that have the same initial letter but may have a different second letter, third letter, and so forth. Understanding and using these skills develop confidence during follow-up word-study sessions introducing guidewords.

Use a dictionary to study guide words: tell students the words are located on the top left of each dictionary page and on the top right of the opposite page. The guide word on the left is the *first word defined* on the page, and the guide word on the right is the *last word defined* on that page. To internalize these skills, some teachers give page numbers randomly so that students race to find guidewords.

Struggling students also want to know how you find a word that "you don't know how to spell." Have students practice by finding a word in the dictionary they do not know how to spell but that they know the initial letters of. Using their phonetic understanding, teachers can help students build confidence by looking up possible spellings and discovering the word wanted. Older students need to also understand the abbreviations for parts of speech, the origins of words, and the different entries with several meanings so that they can apply the correct meaning in sentences.

Clear procedures for simple writing tasks can be helpful for students who do little reading and writing on their own. Writing a report, for example, can seem like a monumental task for students who have difficulty deciphering print. Some suggested procedures for report writing are given below:

1. Have students openly discuss the topic—no wrong or right ideas. Share what they already know about the subject. Write key points on a white board with a colored marker or use an overhead projector. Have students to copy the list of ideas. (Make copies for those who have difficulty copying from the board.)

2. Discuss key parts that are expected in the report (e.g. introduction, body, and conclusion).
3. Have students work with a partner to research online factual information on the subject. Suggest using colored paper to record the names of the sources and key points gathered.
4. Create an outline. Demonstrate how to review notes and decide how to organize and outline the information.
5. Model how to organize thoughts on large cards or on colored paper. (One could place researched notes on a different color of paper.) Arrange ideas that agree with the categories of the outline.
6. Develop the topic sentence or thesis statement for the introductory paragraph and state what the paper will be about. The last statement of the first paragraph should transition to the next paragraph or section.
7. Arrange and discuss all information in each section of the outline and use appropriate transitional phrases to tie the report together.
8. Have students summarize the report by reviewing or restating what they said in the introductory paragraph. Conclude by adding new information that makes the report worthwhile.

Students can edit narratives by using a checklist that includes the following points:

- Check each sentence for correct grammar.
- Check for correct punctuation and capitalization.
- Check for correct spelling of each word.

Transition words and phrases common in reports:

- One thought that comes to mind is—
- When I think about—
- After carefully thinking about—
- After researching the topic, it was evident that—
- When comparing what I knew with what I discovered from research, I found (one, two, three) things that were different (or, were the same).
- In conclusion,—

One group of teachers online used the acronym CUPS (capitalization, usage, punctuation, spelling) to help students remember these writing tips. The suggested pacing guide in Exhibit 8.1a was compiled for kindergarten to fifth grade. Each level builds toward more advanced writing.

Exhibit 8.1a: Pacing Guide for Capitalization, Usage, Punctuation, and Spelling (CUPS): Kindergarten and First Grade

Caps	Usage	Punctuation	Spelling
Capitalize the first letter • in a **sentence**. • of proper nouns such as **names** of people you know and **places** you go. • **days of the week** and **months** in a row.	Re-read (proof read) your writing by reading it aloud. Or, have someone read your work. Check to see if sentences • make sense. • have extra words. • have words left out.	Remember to • put a period (.) at the end of a telling sentence. • put a question mark (?) at the end of a sentence that asks a question. • put an exclamation mark (!) at the end of a sentence to show feelings in writing (e.g. Ouch!)	Spell what the words sounds like when writing ideas for the first time. Then, go back and check words that you were unsure of by using: • the dictionary. • word banks or word lists. • word patterns.

With beginning or reluctant writers, it is important to make writing relevant and necessary for everyday communication and fun. Children can relate to writing a note to Mom, apologizing for forgetting to do a chore. Older children can relate to writing a note to Mom or Dad asking for a certain kind of cell phone, iPhone, iPad, or even special tennis shoes. Through everyday writing, children learn what persuasive writing is and how it is made effective. Second- and third-graders incorporate these continuous writing practices (CUPS) but with more advanced skills. Exhibit 8.1a continued includes these practices for capitalization and usage for these grade levels and for grades four and five.

Exhibit 8.1b CUPS: Second and Third Grades

Capitalization	Usage	Punctuation
Most common ways to use capitalization are:	**The rules below will help you check your written work:**	**Use marks correctly**

Capitalization

Most common ways to use capitalization are:

- At the beginning of all types of sentences;
- When writing "I";
- Titles in names (e.g., Mr., Dr., the Honorable)
- Proper nouns (names of particular people, places or things;
- Names of cities and states;
- Names of countries, continents
- Oceans, rivers and lakes;
- Islands and other land forms,
- Days of the week
- Months of the year
- First and important words in titles, books, magazines, movie and songs;
- Clubs, businesses, and organizations.

Usage

The rules below will help you check your written work:

1. Read your work aloud to make sure it sounds correct.
2. Do you have complete sentences?
3. As you read, point at each word to make sure no word is left out.
4. Check to see if your grammar is correct (e.g., subjects and agreeing verbs).

Spelling

To spell well, it is important to remember rules of the language. But if still unsure, check the dictionary or spell check on your computer.

Other resources:
Franklin Speller
Practice pattern spelling
Your personal spelling dictionary or word bank that lists difficult to remember words.

Punctuation

Use marks correctly

The Period (.):
- Use at the end of telling sentences.
- Use after an initial
- Use after an abbreviation

The Comma (,):
- Use between a series of words;
- Use in dates and addresses;
- Use in large numbers (1,000; 2,500, etc.)
- Use between two complete sentences that are joined with a connecting word;
- Use to set off dialogue, or quotes ("Stop!" said Mom.)
- Use after greeting and closing of a letter;
- Use to separate adjectives;

The Apostrophe ('):
- Use in contractions (doesn't);
- Use in single possessives (sister's scarf);
- Use in plural possessives (parents' pledges)

The Question Mark (?):
- Use after a question;
- Use with direct quotes.
- (Remember to put punctuations INSIDE quotation marks. He said, "Have a nice day."

The Exclamation Point (!):
- Use to express strong feelings. Wow!

Exhibit 8.1c CUPS: Fourth and Fifth Grades

Capitalization	Usage
These capitalization rules will help you edit your writing when using— 1. First word of a sentence 2. Names of persons, places or particular things (Michelle Obama, The White House, Statue of Liberty). 3. Titles used with names (Mr., Dr., The Honorable___) 4. Historical Events (Civil Rights Bill) 5. Abbreviations (M.D., PhD.) 6. Businesses and organizations (Primerica Ins., Boy Scouts) 7. Geographic names (planets, oceans, continents, countries) 8. Key words in titles of books, magazines, movies, programs and songs 9. Days of the week (Monday) 10. Months of the year (January)	These usage rules will help edit your writing when you-- 1. Make sure your sentences express a complete thought. 1. Use basic parts of speech in each sentence 2. Leave no key words out. 3. Make sure proper grammar is used. 4. Check for subject/verb agreement. 5. Become familiar with commonly misused words (e.g., can, may).
Punctuation	**Spelling**
• Use after greeting and closing of a letter; • Use to separate adjectives; **The Apostrophe (')**: • Use in contractions (doesn't); • Use in single possessives (sister's scarf); • Use in plural possessives (parents' pledges) **The Question Mark (?)**: • Use after a question; • Use with direct quotes. (Remember to put punctuations INSIDE quotation marks. He said, "Have a nice day." **The Exclamation Point (!)**: • Use to express strong feelings. Wow!	To spell well, it is important to remember rules of the language. But if still unsure, check the dictionary or spell check on your computer. Spell out acronyms in the beginning of the piece American Federation of Teachers (AFT) and the initials only later in the work. Other resources: Franklin Speller Practice pattern spelling Your personal spelling dictionary or word bank that lists difficult to remember words.

Source: Online Teacher Blog, 2010.

Other strategies for encouraging writing include having students write an essay using adjectives that demonstrate they care about a person, thing, or idea or using transition words to describe a daily event. Sometimes struggling writers find writing lessons overly difficult and stressful. To make it less stressful, first work with the entire class to compile a list of adjectives (such as a list of "caring adjectives," see Exhibit 8.2) that students can then use in their writing. Then, give an example of a caring person, such as Martin Luther King Jr., who made personal sacrifices for the civil rights of his race and for the good of mankind (see Exhibit 8.2).

Exhibit: 8.2. CARING ADJECTIVES

Values in Writing Assignments

*Dr. Martin Luther King Jr. was a **free-hearted**, generous man. He gave of his time to better the social and political conditions of black people in general. More than that, he **helped** all people see themselves as instruments of peace and **kindness**. For years, he was **willing** to leave his wife and children to walk for miles demonstrating his **courageous** dedication. He was **committed** to nonviolence in the process of changing attitudes of people who needed to become **kind, nice, and thoughtful** of others.*

*Now, every January we celebrate Martin Luther King Jr. Day as a time to serve others by being **loving**, **caring**, **giving**, and **forgiving** people.*

(This sample essay can be used to show students how the words are used from the vocabulary list. Some words are derivatives [which ones?]. Notice how the words are used in the sentences, and so.)

Forgiving
Giving
Nice
Helpful
Free-hearted
Thoughtful
Honest
Willing
Loving
Courageous
Committed
Kind

Exhibit 8.3 contains a shell for an essay that students can use to create a narrative essay about a day's event using chronological words and phrases.

Exhibit 8.3: The Narrative Essay

Chronological transitional words and phrases

At the beginning of the day _____
Later that afternoon _____
Then _____
Next _____
The day ended when _____

Summary of Chapter Points

- Further attention should be given to school reform and preparing leaders for the twenty-first century.
- Assessing and addressing diversity in the classroom includes recognizing that struggling students need attention to help them develop such skills as use of the dictionary and writing.
- Literacy is developed through both direct teaching strategies and the cooperative efforts of all stakeholders.

Teaching Tips

1. Encourage appreciation for diversity in the classroom through having students work with a partner to discover cultural likenesses and differences for such topics as foods, family activities, customs, and fun things to do.
2. Use the narrative essay format (Exhibit 8.3) to guide students in using transitional words to write a description of events based on pictures that represent a logical sequence. For example, scramble pictures that show sequential events or chronology, a baby in a crib; a toddler playing with a ball; a cheerleader leading cheers at a high-school football game..

3. Engage students in a game of charades where they pull a caring or other type adjective from a box and demonstrate facial expressions and bodily movements for others to guess the adjective (for example, words such as *smile, frown, cry*).

Suggested Readings/Resources

Allen, N. M. 2012. *When teaching gets tough: Smart ways to reclaim your game*. Alexandria, VA: ASCD.

Dougherty, E. 2012. *Assignments matter: making the connection that help students meet standards*. Alexandria, VA: ASCD.

Fisher, D., and N. Frey. 2010. *Guided instruction: How to develop confident and successful learners*. Alexandria, VA: ASCD.

Hurford, D. M. 1998. *To read or not to read*. New York: A Lisa Drew Book/Scribner.

Kame'enui, E. J., D. W. Carnine, R. C. Dixon, D. C. Simmons, and M. D. Coyne. 2002. *Effective teaching strategies that accommodate diverse learners*. 2nd ed. Columbus, OH: Merrill Prentice Hall.

UNESCO Education Sector. n.d. Retrieved on January 8, 2012, from http://unesdoc.unesco.org/images/0013/001362/136246e.pdf.

Yousif, A. 2003. *Literacy: An overview of definition and assessment. Paper presented at the UNESCO expect meeting: Developing an operational definition of* literacy and a conceptual framework for literacy assessment, Handout. Retrieved from *unesdoc.unesco.org/images/0014/001401/140125eo.pdf*

CHAPTER 9

Action Research: Techniques to Help Teachers Instruct Students with Dyslexia

Chapter Subheadings
Case Reports
Problem-Based Learning and Action Research
Action Research: Standards-Based Project

OBJECTIVE:
To demonstrate the value of problem-based learning and to model a format to follow action research.

TERMS to KNOW

Action research: a form of investigation often used by educators to seek answers to instructional problems and to improve professional practice.

Problem-based learning: student-centered group-learning process using scenarios to solve problems

Teacher preparation programs are the main conduit for preparing a teacher candidate for in-service teaching. Clinical experience is one of the main components of a teacher preparation program. It gives teacher candidates a chance to practice teaching skills in all subject areas including reading and an opportunity to instruct students with varied learning styles and abilities. However, there is support in the literature that teacher preparation programs are not adequately addressing the concept of reading development . From a scientifically based research perspective, thus, some preservice teachers feel unprepared to effectively address all elements of the reading process (Washburn, Joshi, and Cantrell 2011) or to teach students with special needs, including students with dyslexia.

Surveys of teacher knowledge, reviews of the literature on teacher education, and policy statements indicate that many teachers are underprepared to teach language content and processes to children whose reading and learning problems are language based (Moats and Lyon 1996). Moreover, it is crucial for teachers to understand how dyslexia affects students, to know how to help dyslexics with language difficulties, and to focus on the strengths of students with dyslexia. Authentic experiences during preservice and in-service teaching are beneficial to the successful implementation of strategies and techniques for students with dyslexia.

Accordingly, an action research project conducted during the 2012–2013 school term provided a venue for students enrolled in a graduate reading program to observe students with dyslexia, record findings, and devise and implement lesson plans. The project allowed graduate students (currently certified elementary teachers) to glean best practices for teaching early learners with dyslexia through an action research project. Initially, graduate students were provided with descriptive information about how to best impart instruction with students with dyslexia. Armed with this information, students developed lesson plans that focused on providing instruction for students with dyslexia, especially as it relates to the components of reading (phonics, phonemic awareness, vocabulary, comprehension, and fluency).

Students were instructed to develop or describe a problem they were facing in their respective elementary classrooms that involved early learners ranging from third to sixth grades. They were to discuss a particular early learner's difficulties in mastering skills in comprehension, fluency, phonemic awareness, phonics, or vocabulary. As a result, students developed a thorough lesson plan that contained essential components (i.e., common-core standards known as national standards) and took into consideration the early learner's learning difference. After the aforementioned items were designed, graduate students were then asked to select a colleague (an elementary-school teacher) possessing experience teaching students with dyslexia. This collaboration yielded constructive feedback regarding the quality of the lesson plan in relation to meeting the early learner's needs. Through this constructive feedback, cooperating colleagues revealed their own experiences and/or observations from teaching learners with dyslexia. Ensuing questions included:

- Which instructions given in the lesson plan relate best to students with dyslexia?
- Which activities or instructions best utilize a multisensory teaching approach (i.e., look, hear, say, write)?

- What alternatives to reading text are offered to the student (e.g., audiotape, CDs, debates)?
- What strategies and activities are geared to utilizing the student's memory?
- What alternatives for written tests and assignments are offered?
- How does the plan include sequential steps in activities?
- How are confidence builders infused?
- How are the components of reading emphasized in the lesson plan?
- Explain how the alignment among goals and objectives, activities and assessment of students are consistent.

The following five case reports include scenarios, excerpts of lesson plans, and constructive feedback from teachers of students with dyslexia. These cases were developed by individual teachers, and shared with their colleagues for discussion.

Case Reports

Case 1 reported that her third-grade student had problems transferring words onto paper. She noticed that his skills in comprehension and phonics were not at a third-grade level. Her efforts included making sure that he understood what was asked of him by having him repeat directions. She paired him with a peer and gave him a copy of the lesson to take home for reinforcement. Independent practice allowed the student to work with peers in a small-group setting, listen to audiotapes, and discover words that were discussed previously in the lesson.

According to constructive feedback from her cooperating colleague, the teacher had changed her lesson plan to enhance the learning level of all students by incorporating all learning styles. In addition to reading text, the teacher incorporated audiotapes, peer tutoring, and small-group instruction. The struggling student's memory was ehanced by the teacher's strategy of repeating directions and modeling the lesson.

Case 2 reported that her third-grade student had difficulty with fluency and problems linking individual words together. This caused a lack of comprehension. The student would act out in class and constantly interrupt the class when other students read aloud. The lesson included conducting a readers' theater to promote fluency and comprehension. *A reader's theater is an integrated approach for involving students in reading, writing, listening, and speaking activities. It involves children in sharing literature, reading aloud, writing scripts, performing with a purpose, and working collaboratively* (Cornwell 2015).

After a thorough explanation of what was expected from the students, the teacher allowed students to work in small groups, and in one-to-one pairs to practice their respective lines . The student with dyslexia participated in choral reading and paired reading with the teacher to build confidence. The objectives of the lesson were met and addressed state standards of interpreting text through moving, drawing, speaking, acting, or singing.

Constructive feedback from the cooperating colleague revealed that the teacher provided numerous opportunities for students to gain the courage to read aloud to their peers. The teacher explained fluency and its importance in the process of reading. She also provided thorough instructions for the assessment and modeled a readers' theater.

Case 3 reported that her twelve-year-old fifth-grade student read at a third-grade level. He struggled with reading comprehension and vocabulary. The strategies employed by the elementary teacher included repeating directions to ensure comprehension. A class routine, charts, and calendars were given to students to outline key terms and concepts. The students were also encouraged to use graphic organizers and calendars to record assessment dates and homework assignments. According to the devised lesson plan, students were grouped based on the reading abilities, allowing them to move at a pace comparable to their respective abilities. One-on-one tutoring was available for students in need of extra help. Assessments were modified to accommodate struggling students to ensure content mastery and aid the students in performing to their abilities. Students were able to concentrate on the targeted content.

The cooperating colleague reported that targeted, students tend to read directions over and over, eventually asking for assistance. She also shared that the older the student, the less responsive he or she became. Her constructive feedback was that the teacher should use a graphic organizer – one that has a key word in the center, and related words spider out. She asserted that the teacher's activities and assessments were consistent as the students assisted the teacher in completing a sample bubble map (graphic organizer), and eventually created a bubble map independent of the teacher to demonstrate understanding of a main character and his traits.

Case 4 reported that she had an eight-year-old third-grade student who had difficulty with consonant-vowel-consonant (CVC) words; the teacher further mentioned that a major part of the student's difficulty involved a working memory. She had problems with long-term memory and recalling grade-level sight words. She could say the sounds of letters but had a possible visual discrimination problem. The student's difficulty with grade-level vocabulary had an impact on her comprehension and capabilities and her ability to learn the meaning of new words from context. The teacher's goal was to create a plan that focused on the growth of the student's vocabulary in an effort to enhance her ability to infer meaning while reading.

The teacher used different colored highlighters, repeatedly reminded students of rules and instructions, and provided one-on-one support. According to the cooperating colleague, all these strategies relate well to students with dyslexia and are geared to enhancing the student's memory. The teacher also had the student listen to a CD and participate in a matching game, using cards to find short vowel sounds. A star was awarded to the student when she created short vowels, which built her confidence.

Case 5 reported that a third-grade student with dyslexia could not read at the same pace as his peers. He had difficulty putting sounds together to form simple and complex words. The student also seemed unable to remember words that he saw previously and struggled to sound out every word. Phonics and phonemic awareness skills were lacking.

In an effort to provide instruction to this student, the teacher constructed a lesson that focused on phonics generalizations. For example, the teacher asked students to circle all words that have an *r*-controlled sound (i.e., car, girl, church). After the students circled their words, students shared their words by writing them on the board. The teacher closed the phonics lesson by discussing the seven phonic generalizations. The teacher reinforced the lesson by saying a word and asking students to identify which of the seven rules applied to that word.

The action research project resulted in graduate students creating lesson plans and activities that demonstrated strategies that are most helpful for struggling readers. The plans and activities exhibited sensitivity to various learning styles. Teachers emphasized solutions for students with areas of weakness while providing whole-group instruction. Teachers also provided positive reinforcement for students with dyslexia. These results mirrored the meaning of a statement Malcolm Alexander (Strategies for Teachers 2013) shared about a teacher who said, "When I teach, when I look at a student's work, I always try to find something nice in it. And then go into it" (Sparkling new ideas section, para. 1). For good results in teaching, the following general recommendations were presented in an online publication of the University of Michigan:

1. During times when students are independently working on class work, give students the option to work in a study carrel with headphones to eliminate distractions.
2. Allow extra time to complete tests.
3. Provide a regular study buddy whom the student sits next to in class.
4. Give "think time" before answering a question. This can be done by presenting a question and then pausing or by coming back to the student after a little while and repeating the question. Alternatively, have multiple students answer the same question. In this way, several models are provided.
5. Provide opportunities for writing and spelling every day, in a variety of formats, such as writing in a journal, sending an e-mail, writing or copying a list of homework activities, writing on a large wall calendar, writing thank you letters, or archiving items in a collection.
6. Explicitly teach organization and planning skills for completing and tracking homework. Instruct students how to break down large projects into smaller tasks.

7. Improve word retrieval for naming through participation in one or more of these games: Scattegories, Taboo, Guesstures, Password, Scrabble, logic puzzles, rebus puzzles, Catch-Phrase, UpWords, Tribond, Plexers, crossword puzzles, and other word puzzles.
8. Facilitate phonemic awareness for blending, segmenting, deletion, and discrimination tasks. Earobics software addresses each of these areas in a highly motivating context.
9. Give manipulatives (things to touch and move around) whenever possible to work on math related to time, money, or fractions.
10. Explicitly and systematically teach math to students with dyslexia (including models of proficient problem solving, verbalization of thought processes, guided practice, corrective feedback, and frequent cumulative review). *Dyslexia and Mathematics* (1992, 2nd ed.), edited by T. R. Miles and Elaine Miles, and The Institute of Education Sciences (IES) *Guide for Assisting Students Struggling with Mathematics: Response to Intervention (RtI)* for Elementary and Middle Schools provide more information (Strategies for Teaching 2013, general recommendations section, para. 1).

Problem-Based Learning and Action Research

Aside from action research projects, problem-based learning (PBL) is another strategy that may be employed in teacher preparation programs. This strategy would allow preservice teachers to work together in discovering a resolution to specific problems encountered when teaching students with dyslexia. When preservice teachers are presented with an authentic, specific scenario, they may rely on their knowledge to begin navigating toward a solution. Acquired knowledge, critical thinking, collaboration with other students, and facilitation by the instructor would guide preservice teachers through this student-centered, group-learning process known as problem-based learning. PBL would simulate a team approach (much like real school settings) to address students with dyslexia. Moreover, the aforementioned cases could be transformed into PBL scenarios. Students would then apply their knowledge and resources to arrive at a solution for a student's successful outcome.

Considering an apparent lack of collaboration of special educators and general educators in the redesign of teacher preparation programs, it would be beneficial to consider a collaborative approach for designing, implementing, and monitoring the field experiences of teacher education candidates or preservice teachers. These field experiences can serve as a major catalyst to action research projects that further the awareness and understanding of teaching students with dyslexia. A fruitful collaboration will explore deficits in teacher preparation as it relates to preservice teachers' capacity to instruct students with dyslexia. Elements of the action research project include the following:

1. Survey recent graduates (currently teaching) in an effort to glean perceptions of the teacher preparation program's strengths and/or weaknesses related to being prepared to teach students with dyslexia.
2. General and special-education faculty should discuss standards and best practices significant to the development of well-informed teachers of students with dyslexia; for example, developing and implementing an individual education plan (IEP) to include response to intervention (RTI).
3. Action research projects should be designed to guide, inform, and enhance and to promote reflection of how instruction is provided for students with dyslexia. Special-education and general-education majors should collectively and simultaneously conduct action research projects to include observing, designing, and implementing lesson plans and assessing students. Two focus groups should discuss the action research projects with faculty members.
4. Support from K–12 schools (administrators and cooperating teachers) should be sought in order to provide an authentic and engaging training ground for teacher education candidates or preservice teachers.
5. Reading course objectives and activities should be redesigned with influence from special educators, national standards, and common-core standards.
6. Upon participants' graduation and during the first two years of placement, faculty should administer a survey to determine if the action research project had a positive impact on preparing teacher candidates to teach students with dyslexia.

Fostering collaborations is paramount among general and special-education teachers as they contribute to the school community through both direct and indirect services to support struggling students, children with disabilities, other educators who work with them, and their families (ASHA 2006). This action research project is a perfect context to facilitate the collaborative process between elementary education teachers and special-education teachers.

According to Moats (2009), there are far too few cross-disciplinary programs in language and literacy. Substantive study of language structure and language learning is often unavailable to those being credentialed in reading and special education, although there should be substantial common ground in the training of general and special educators. This type of training and specialized action research to accompany it is needed in contemporary teacher preparation programs.

Action Research: Standards-Based Project

The results of a standards-based research project conducted in an urban school district in central Mississippi are noteworthy. Although the demographics of the district are similar to those of many other urban districts around the country, test scores on the Mississippi Curriculum Test indicate that most students (approximately 80 percent) were performing at or above the *proficiency level* for the state. The *proficiency level* in 2007 was interpreted as *above average* (B).

The research project included observations of school personnel involved in professional development. Regarding school leadership and administration, it appeared that the administrators attended professional development training along with the teachers in their respective schools. School administrators and teachers in the school district were fairly consistent in their common perceptions of interventions and instruction needed for struggling readers. In addition, school administrators tended to follow district procedures when identifying and supporting the literacy needs of struggling readers. The literacy intervention found to be most effective among teachers was *direct, systematic phonics instruction*. This intervention is research based and meets the standards proposed by the National Research Panel and other similar research groups.

Observations and the use of diagnostic assessments were guided by the following standards:

1. Learning differences should be diagnosed as soon as parents and/or teachers realize there is a learning difficulty so that appropriate interventions can be made.
2. The acquisition of letter-sound relationships and their function in reading and spelling words should be assessed.
3. Reading passages should be used as a natural function that occurs when the proper mental stimulation has occurred.
4. School administrators and teachers should be trained to produce positive results when all have been trained with common goals and methodologies strategic for student achievement.

The results of the observations provided supportive data that standards-based teaching and learning enhance student achievement.

Several implications from the observations emerged. Among them were that effective teaching is a result of teacher empowerment. Teachers become educational collaborators through social media and educational blogs along with strategic in-service and professional development training. Teachers must be responsive to the variety of ways students learn; therefore, teachers should examine the learning styles of students in ways that can be used to inform instruction. Additionally, teachers should keep students and parents apprised of progress, trigger special support for students who need it, and evaluate ongoing instructional practices.

Teacher education departments at colleges and universities should collaborate closely with various external stakeholders to better prepare preservice teachers to meet the needs of students in the "real world." Educational institutions must also be prepared to train administrators and teachers for a diverse student population that is struggling to survive in the current global society. Many young educators do not believe they currently have the diverse skills necessary to succeed in the multicultural classrooms of today.

More than a decade ago, the US government conducted a $14 million study of adult literacy that extended over a five-year period. In September of 1993, this agency conducted lengthy interviews of over 26,700 adults statistically balanced for age, gender, ethnicity, education level, and location (urban, suburban and rural). This research was designed to represent the United States as a whole. Involving twelve states across the United States, this study found that 21 to 23 percent of adult Americans were not "able to locate information in a text," could not "make low-level inferences using printed materials," and were unable to "integrate easily identifiable pieces of information" (US Department of Education, Office of Educational Research and Improvement 2002). About ten years later, findings from research for the Consortium on Reading Excellence showed that 47 percent of adults, about twice as many adults as earlier, were unable to locate information in a text or complete a job application.

In view of these findings and implications from the standards-based research project, there is a need to build upon these findings and recommend changes for the future. Therefore, the following recommendations are made for engagement in action research and other professional development practices:

1. Engage all teachers in professional development that focuses on reading and language skills to further ensure *thoughtful literacy* (higher-level thinking, communicating, and applying concepts) across the curriculum with follow up onsite to monitor application and implementation.
2. Train teachers and include modeling of lessons or demonstrations on presenting subject area concepts for struggling students.
3. Allow time for teacher reflections, feedback, and evaluations during professional development trainings and enrichment sessions.
4. Use these evaluations to strategically plan and implement future trainings in areas of need, such as the five components of literacy instruction: phonics, vocabulary, spelling, comprehension, reading fluency, and writing.
5. Train teachers to identify learning difficulties in the components of literacy and provide professional development in appropriate methods to assess students for strengths and weaknesses.
6. Recruit qualified teachers who are team players and are willing to collaborate with colleagues when determining best practices for pre-assessment, instruction, and post-assessment.
    a.

2. Invite experts to present the theoretical underpinnings of teaching and learning to teachers and school administrators so that they will have common understandings of instructional expectations and student achievement.
    c. Prepare mentors for the mentor-teacher partnership by offering training in the area of mentoring along with new teacher-training sessions. Then, provide mentors for new teachers to ensure that positive experiences happen early in their teaching career.
    d. Take advantage of colleges' and universities' community service trainings, conferences, and consultants in addressing various educational issues.
    e. Promote regular collaboration with parents and other community stakeholders to create a learning community with authentic incentives for students, motivation for academic achievement, and total development for all students regardless of circumstances or their innate abilities.

Summary of Chapter Points

- Action research improves understanding of strategies for enhancing the performance of struggling learners with dyslexia. It is hoped that many negative perceptions about dyslexia will be erased as teachers engage in action research to reflect on their practice.
- It is hoped that those who perceive dyslexia as a unique gift that needs to be cultivated will continue to share lessons learned to guide the practice of others.
- As a result, readers who are dyslexic will understand better how to adjust their learning style to include reading strategies that will enhance their gifts that extend well beyond language deficiencies.
- It is hoped that people with related reading difficulties will focus less on their diagnoses and more on the strengths of their style of reading and learning.

Teaching Tips

Participate in a professional development activity provided through a college or local school district. Note if any of the activities relate to instructing diverse learners who have dyslexic characteristics. As part of an action research project, write up proposed steps to follow for observing a classroom; as part of the project, provide debriefings for the strategies observed.

Suggested Readings/Resources

Dyslexia Help. 2013. "Strategies for teachers: Sparking new ideas for your classroom. Dyslexia Help: Success Starts Here." Retrieved from http://dyslexiahelp.umich.edu/professionals/dyslexia-school/strategies-for-teachers.

Moats, L. C., and G. R. Lyon. 1996. "Wanted: Teachers with knowledge of language." *Topics in Language Disorders* 16(2): 73–86.

Redford, K. n.d. "Dyslexics & 'real world' learning." The Yale Center for Dyslexia & Creativity. Retrieved from http://dyslexia.yale.edu/EDU_projectbasedlearning.html.

Stevens, A. 2010. "3 ways teachers can help dyslexic students: Pt. 2-overcoming difficulties." *ReadingHorizons* (blog), July 26. Retrieved from www.readinghorizons.com/blog/post/2010/07/26/3-Ways-Teachers-Can-Help-Dyslexic-Students-Pt-2-Overcoming-Reading-Difficulties.aspx.

Resource Section

In this book, we share current research-based strategies to support students who have specific learning differences. Obviously, teachers and school administrators need ongoing professional development activities and appropriate resources to meet the diverse needs of their respective student population. This section identifies resources and websites that can assist teachers in keeping abreast of current best strategies to help modify instruction and accommodate struggling students with learning differences.

Additionally, the purpose of this book is to emphasize that the needs of struggling readers urgently need to be addressed. Research sources we reviewed generally agreed that one in five students is a struggling reader. One in ten will likely be unable to read effectively without direct instruction or special interventions. Teachers and school administrators have recognized that the increasing number of students who are referred to special education is indicative of an increase in reading deficiencies. Yet, in many cases, neither the referring teachers nor the special-education teachers have found a solution to address these discovered reading difficulties. With the level of accountability required by No Child Left Behind, school administrators cannot pass the responsibility primarily to teachers.

School administrators must also document collaborative efforts and resources made available to teach every child regardless of disabilities or circumstances. Many school leaders develop a school action plan. Because professional development is crucial for teachers to stay current in regard to best practices, professional development encompasses all types of learners, ranging from those who struggle to those who are ready for grade-level and advanced work.

Teaching the Whole Child: Procedures and Forms for Making Accommodations
Online resources at www.fcrr.org and www.fcrr.org/activities are free to all schools, principals, and teachers. The action plan that follows is the result of collaboration among school administrators, principals, and teachers. (Permission is granted to access

this plan from the website, and educators may adapt it as needed.) A school's action plan should also outline possible indicators a school district can utilize. Usually, a *strategic planning team* is established to study the needs of all students and staff.

Exhibit RS.1: Action Plan Outline for Building a Successful

School-Wide Intervention System

A Principal's Action Plan for Building a Successful School-wide Intervention Program			
Common Traits of Successful Schools	Characteristic	Specific Feature	Observable Result **Successful Principals will...**
Strong Leadership	Knowledgeable	Recognize and identify all student needs	• Determine and establish: • intervention budget needs • reading instruction as a priority **Provide:** • Scheduling needs • Sufficient staff
		Maintain basic knowledge of research-based programs and their availability	• Locate research-based programs for teachers to guide intervention • Allocate funding for research-based programs • Match program to student need
		Data interpretation	• Conduct and lead data meetings
		Recognize and identify teacher and scheduling needs	**Determine and establish:** • Reading instructions as a priority
			• ample time for reading instruction in small groups
			• time on task as a priority
			• supply teacher support for problem solving and success
	Strong Vision	Provide, clearly explain, and describe vision for	• establish mottos; belief statements; expectations

RS 1 Continue

Positive Belief	Beliefs about success with all students and teacher dedication	High expectations	**Provide:** • Support to help teachers meet expectation • Motivational workshops • Research pointing to high performing, high poverty schools
Data Analysis	Ongoing data management and utilization	Data structures, disaggregation, and mobilization	**Attend monthly grade-level data meetings:** • to learn about school intervention needs • to make changes to personnel and/or programming **Scaffold teachers and staff to:** • discuss and share ideas about student progress • follow up in classroom with differentiated instruction • use data management systems to accurately and effectively analyze data
Common Traits of Successful Schools	**Characteristic**	**Specific Features**	**Observable Result Successful Principals will...**
Effective Scheduling	Efficient	Flexible use of time, staff, and resources	**Arrange for:** • most appropriate provides of small group instruction • prioritize responsibilities and skills across staff and instructional personnel • common teacher planning time by grade-level • an uninterrupted reading block of 90 minutes or more • identify specific times when iii will be provided

RS 1 continue

Professional Development	Differentiated	On-going and Follow-up	Recognize and establish: • ongoing/follow-up training for veteran teachers • on-going/follow-up training for new teachers • problem of high teacher turnover rate and create a contingency plan for high turnover rates • building and district level people to provide training • time in school scheduled to regular (monthly/weekly) training
Scientifically Based Intervention Programs	Targeted	Differentiate materials for more precise lesson planning A set scope and sequence focusing on a specific reading component Different components of reading addressed Technology-based reinforcement	• locate research-based intervention programs for teachers to guide instruction • allocate funding for research-based intervention programs • strategically select intervention programs based on student needs
Parent Involvement	Initiative in Communication	Flexible and accommodating	Provide: • babysitting services at parent information nights • provide food at parent • information nights • provide multiple parent information sessions – one in the morning hours and one in the evening • information in multiple • languages • interpreters at parent meetings • Establish structures to: • nurture parental relationships • involve students in their own learning, take ownership of their learning

Intervention strategies may include paraprofessionals as tutors and teacher aides along with instructional and learning specialists to help provide the necessary interventions and accommodations for different learners. Second, the planning team may be expanded to form a *core team* that includes parents, teachers, principals, the school board, school district administrators, local city leaders, and community constituents. Additionally, before screening or testing a student, it is required by school law to inform parents of the student's needs. This can be done in the form of a letter or a special form to be signed by the parent or guardian, granting permission to proceed with the evaluation. A sample letter to parents requesting permission to test is presented here.

Exhibit RS.2: Sample Letter: Permission to Test

(Date)

Dear (Parent's name)

You have expressed some concerns about your child's reading skills. In order to better understand how we can help your child improve, an individualized screening is recommended. One of the purposes of this evaluation will be to determine if _____ has a learning style that will require a different teaching style or strategy that is not currently being used. The screening will take from one to two hours. The curriculum/screening facilitators will be happy to share the results with you about two weeks after the date of screening.

If you have any questions, please contact the coordinator by telephone at _____, or the school's principal at your child's school. In order to proceed with the screening, your permission is necessary. Please sign and return this letter, as indicated below, to the school not later than the day of the test.

_____

Parent/Guardian

Sincerely,

_____

(Signature of principal or counselor)

Return to facilitator of screening/testing for reading difficulties. (Check one of the statements below. Request a completed copy of this letter for your records.)

-------- I give permission for my child _____ to be screened for uncommon reading difficulties that may need extra reading interventions.
-------- I do not give my permission for this screening.

Parent's signature: _____ Date: _____

Address: _____ City/Zip: _____

Telephone #: _____ Cell/or Emergency _____

Exhibit RS.2: Rationale for Universal Screening
The checklist form for which permission is requested is found in chapter 4. The sample action plan provided here was designed to address the needs of regular students and struggling readers, especially those with dyslexic tendencies. Regular students are also supported through the Tiers 1, 2, and 3 of the instructional program. And since dyslexia is considered a regular education language difference—not usually ruled as requiring special education—the strategies can be utilized by the majority of regular education students. The multisensory strategies that are used to teach dyslexic students are also welcomed by nondyslexic students. Regular students, especially those with gaps in their reading understandings, often find it helpful if they can apply the rules of spelling to reading multisyllabic words and to understanding a variety of texts. However, the speed at which concepts are taught to dyslexic students is usually too slow for regular education students, who can get it after one or two reviews and applications.

Reading methods that speed through reading concepts aimed at the majority of students who have no major language or spelling problems, comprising 80 percent of the class, will not usually be effective with struggling dyslexic students. The student with reading/language disabilities would have difficulty understanding reading strategies normally outlined in the basal readers with timed and tested units. For measurable success, teachers should stress rules for each new concept and focus on one concept at a time. In each lesson, opportunities to apply the concept should be presented at least seven times during the lesson. Struggling readers and different learners need direct, systematic instruction with frequent reviews on the same day. On the following days, systematic reviews should connect previous lessons with new concepts. In other words, students should be able to recite, write, demonstrate, and/or apply learned skills in new settings.

Finally, the interventions and programs used to instruct all kinds of struggling readers must be research based and multisensory. The multisensory approach could also be called differentiated instruction because both approaches allow for differences. If students lack competency in any one of the components of reading before third grade, there will be gaps in the literacy process. One in eight will survive the challenges of reading success through the grades (Juel 2001). Most of these students will likely struggle with reading and learning throughout adulthood if appropriate interventions are not provided for success in school and in life. Many schools collaborate with key personnel to establish a school-wide action plan (universal screening) similar to the 504 Plan that assess learning needs and differences.

About the 504 Plan

Teachers are often concerned about and frustrated with students who appear to be above average in intelligence but who are unsuccessful in the regular classroom—ranging from forgetting or losing assignments to an inability to respond properly to language-based assignments. For example, upper elementary and secondary students may leave homework in their desks or turn in incomplete homework. Parents also have expressed frustration when they observe their children working diligently for an hour or more on a fifteen-minute assignment. A dyslexic student can be taught a spelling or language skill from Monday through Thursday, but there is still no guarantee that the student will remember the skill on Friday. Students with characteristics of dyslexia also tend to freeze up and panic during tests.

Frequently in the regular classroom, dyslexic children suffer in many ways. If the teacher lacks understanding of the students' learning process, the educator may see the student as slow and unmotivated. These misconceptions may translate to low self-esteem of the dyslexic student. Once there is understanding of the dyslexic student and the learning process, there are some ways to help the dyslexic student in the classroom. Chapter 2 contains explanations of content that can be included in categories of the sample 504 Plan that follows.

Exhibit RS.3: Sample 504 Plan

There are three major areas unique to dyslexia students that should be the focus of a 504 Plan:

I. Teaching strategies for students with auditory-linguistic differences
II. Teaching strategies for students with visual-spatial behaviors
III. Teaching strategies for students with differences in a combination of auditory-visual and spatial behaviors

Auditory-linguistic students will find that auditory materials are easier to retain and understand. Some can hear a story told and retell the entire story accurately but cannot write the responses that he or she made orally. Some even have auditory-linguistic and visual-spatial differences combined. In such cases, the main methods of compensation would be:

(1) Make auditory material easier to hear and understand through visual aids.
(2) Develop strong visual skills by showing and telling.

1. **Exhibit RS.4: Tips for Helping the Severely Struggling Student in the Regular Classroom**
   a. **Accentuate the positive:** Accentuating the positive increases the dyslexic student's motivation. Dyslexic students learn differently. If there is a certain assignment that is completed, yet not presented as instructed, be sure to accentuate positively the correct parts first: "You certainly have made a great start, but I am sure you want to include—" This will help stimulate the student in a constructive way. By reviewing the requirements in a positive way will provide corrective instruction without frustration.
   b. **Be understanding:** Understanding your student's needs is important. Many times the dyslexic student may appear unmotivated or slow. Due to lack of understanding these misconceptions can lead to frustration and low self-esteem. If the educator understands the learning process in the dyslexic person, this can help the student's self-esteem, as the student will realize that the teacher understands his or her particular circumstances.
   c. **Communicate with your students:** Communication leads to academic improvement; schedule frequent meetings with your students. Talk about their improvement, and where they may need improvement. Ask your students what learning techniques may work best for them. Communicating with your students helps their self-confidence and motivation.
   d. **Develop a plan:** Developing a plan can help the student set goals. Sitting down with your students, and developing a plan will help them to achieve their goals. Helping your students achieve their goals will help them to realize their capabilities and increase motivation for learning. These four tips will help the dyslexic student's experience in the classroom. If the educator understands the dyslexic student and incorporates these tips there is a possibility of improvement in the student.
   e. **Encourage:** Encourage your student. Having a learning disability can be a frustrating process. We all know a little encouragement can go a long way.
   f. **Follow up:** Schedule a time with your students so you can evaluate their progress. During this time allow your students to express concerns about learning and classroom work. Make sure they conduct a self-evaluation. This will enable them to understand and analyze their learning process.
   g. **Goals:** Set goals for your students and allow them to set goals for themselves. Once the goals are set, give your students a time frame. Once the goals are met, meet with your students and discuss their progress. This will allow your students to understand the importance of planning, goal setting, and organization. Set both long-term and short-term goals.
   h. **Homework:** Do your homework. Dyslexia is a learning disability. Be sure as an educator you do your research and understand the learning process

of the dyslexic student. Don't limit yourself to the age range that you are teaching; understand that you are helping your student develop into adulthood and that part of your responsibility, along with the parent, is to nourish and educate a successful individual.

i. **Intelligence:** Explain to your students the different types of intelligence. Emphasize the strong points of the particular type of their intelligence. Allow your students to complete projects geared toward their intelligence. This will boost your students' self-esteem.

j. **Journal:** Journaling can help everyone. Tell your students to journal. Ask them to write about their goals, accomplishments, and fears. Teach them that their journal is a safe place to express themselves without fear, judgment, or ridicule. This will improve their writing and creativity.

k. **Knowledge:** Knowledge never ends. Encourage students to think outside the box. Tell them that knowledge never ends. There is always room for growth and knowledge.

l. **Love:** Teach your students to love themselves and know that they are loved. At a young age, children tend to judge themselves by their grades; encourage their talents and character development as a person. Tell your students that it is important to do their best, but at the same time, a letter defines no one. Encourage parents to teach this at home.

After teachers and parents have utilized the tips, it is important to know how to adapt the report card to reflect classroom accommodations. Too often we hear teachers comment, "I can't make a difference among my students." In real life, accommodations are made for people with talent as well as for people with handicaps. Dyslexia is a hidden disability, and to the person who has to deal with this learning difference on a daily basis, it is just as real as a physical handicap. The following are some auditory and visual strategies for the struggling student.

Auditory Learner's Strategies

- Read out loud to yourself. It will help you to understand and remember better.
- Be sure you *pronounce* words the right way, and be sure you hear what is said correctly. If in doubt, ask for the word or sentence to be pronounced by the teacher.
- Get permission to ask someone else if you do not understand directions or material.
- Learn how to repeat directions to yourself and follow them, underlining segments as you go. When possible, put the directions in your own

words—that means that you understand them (especially do this with test questions).
- Learn to listen for key information. Pick out the how and the five Ws: who, what, when, where, and why.
- If blending sounds or syllables together in words is hard, ask for some one-on-one help with this. You can't read all spelling words easily if you don't hear them correctly.
- Older students sometimes have to write notes that the teacher dictates. If this is hard, ask the teacher for permission to do the following.
  - Use a recorder for class reviews or important information. Then then you can play it back at home—quietly and slowly—for better understanding. Be sure to add *missed* information to your own notes.
  - Get a carbon or reproduced copy of another student's notes to use as a backup to your own. This will help you to get material you missed and perhaps help you to learn how to take better notes yourself.
  - Borrow the teacher's notes to copy and compare to yours.

All this will help you and allow you to listen better when the teacher is talking. But you should continue to learn how to become a good note taker.

Visual Learner's Strategies

- Use written materials as much as possible.
  a. Ask for study sheets and outlines.
  b. Follow in the book as the teacher reads or discusses.
  c. Draw a "picture" of information as you hear it (ask your teacher about mapping).
  d. Use pictures, maps, and charts in your textbooks to help you understand.
  e. Put little visual reminders on your desk or in a notebook: math charts, number lines, vowel-sound pictures, parts of speech—or your own special shortcut tricks or formulas that will trigger your memory.
- Buy your own textbooks so you can mark them up—write notes in the margins or number important items.
- Make pictures in your head about what someone is saying or what you are supposed to do.
- Use games and handmade flash cards to learn. Buy blank flashcards or cut up index cards. Write questions/words on one card, the answers on another, and then match-up cards. Great for vocabulary words, science terms, study questions, and so on.

- Fold notebook paper in half lengthwise. Write the question or vocabulary word on left side, answer or word definition on right side. Fold paper to quiz yourself.
- Ask people to *show* you things or *demonstrate* how do to something (e.g., ask them to work through a math problem with you so you understand the steps).
- *Look* at people when they talk: "read" their lips.
- Write things down.
    a. Use colors to help you see things better. Highlight the parts of the text: one color for vocabulary words, another for the main idea, and so on. But be careful: don't color the whole page.
    b. Think of shorthand ways to write directions, such as I C U B4 U C me (get it?).
    c. Use a little self-stick notepad to jot down page numbers, and so on. Keep one in your desk.

Tips for Parents

- Give your child a lot of opportunities for individual learning/teaching.
    a. Use new words and include his or her vocabulary words in conversation.
    b. Give alternate, more descriptive words. If your child says, "That was great," you say, "That was *interesting*" or "That was *awesome*."
    c. Correct pronunciation of words by carefully repeating the word correctly.
    d. Play word games such as jumping on word cards on the floor when called. Purchase commercial word games, such as Scrabble or crossword puzzle books.
    e. Ask your child to explain meanings and concepts to you to help enhance understanding.
- Have your child practice retelling sequenced events, such as stories or plots of TV shows.
- Regardless of grade level, read to your child. For younger children, occasionally insert an incorrect word, phrase, or nonsense sentence and see if they can catch the mistake.
- Check your child's word understanding. Does your child understand the concept of rhyming words, opposites, and analogies. (grass is green and sugar is ___)? Does he or she understand the hidden meanings of idioms (sharp as a tack) and jokes or riddles? We often assume a child understands these word meanings when he or she doesn't. For support, check out online sources like "ELS Idioms," by David Oliver (2007).

- Spatial words, often prepositions, are a common problem. Does your child know the meaning of *between, next to, before, after*? These can really affect following directions. Demonstrate prepositions by using a basketball and have your child describe where the ball goes in a basketball game. Any game ball can be used for this kind of demonstration.
- Record your child's incorrect words, phrases, or sentence structure. Play back recordings and help him or her correct the language.
- If you child has sound blending difficulty, help him or her with this important reading skill.
    - Play "I Spy" with words instead of colors. Say, "I spy c-u-p or a t-a-ble"—breaking words into sounds or syllables. Child must put sounds together to make correct word.
    - Show a picture containing several objects. Name one of the objects (e.g., tr-u-ck) and have your child find the correct object.
    - Give parts of words that your child must finish (e.g., cucum__ or school__).
    - Have your child listen to radio or TV for specific information (e.g., the score of the game, the temperature from the weather report).
    - Encourage your child to listen to sport reporters and record the colorful metaphors and descriptions of player performance.
- Below are examples of auditory processing problems: know which ones most affect your child.
    - **Auditory discrimination:** has trouble hearing slight differences in sounds and gives incorrect responses (e.g., lawn, long; chip, trip; ten, tin).
    - **Auditory memory:** has trouble remembering things heard and therefore has difficulty listening and following directions.
    - **Auditory sequencing:** has trouble remembering things in order: a sequence of events or sequential sounds in words.
    - **Auditory figure-ground:** has trouble hearing specific sounds over background noise or paying attention; hears only parts of words or sentences.
    - **Auditory lag:** thinks or responds slowly because all of the above are confusing and take time!

How Teachers Can Help

- Allow students to ask each other for confirmation or explanation of material they may have missed or not understood. This should be a prearranged agreement with targeted students to avoid embarrassment or disruption.
- Give struggling students a little extra time to respond.
- Provide a visual example with any verbal directions or explanations (e.g., write on the board or use pictures, use an overhead projector or smart board).

- Be sure to teach and discuss the vocabulary needed for a specific task or subject.
- Check knowledge of other word concepts (see "Tips for Parents").
- Speak slowly, giving simple, uncluttered directions. Give instructions in sequence when possible.
- Face students when speaking, so they can *see* you talking.
- Relate to prior information presented in past concepts and/or experiences. Give correct examples and discuss to help enhance memory.
- Teach students short songs or poems—one line at a time.
- Make frequent checks for comprehension. The child should put the lesson in his or her own words.
- Don't assume that all the students understand the material/concepts presented verbally: they may have missed parts of them. To check, ask them to repeat key points.
- **Oral work**. Allow students to choose how they will make presentations rather than require only lengthy oral reports. Let targeted students use notes or visual aids.
- **Note taking**. See suggestions for note taking under "Auditory Learner's Strategies."
- **Be sure the student is hearing correct words**. Some common errors:
    a. **Word endings.** The student may leave off the last letter of the root word: help him or her to say the root or base word before putting on the ending.
    b. **Ending blends.** The student may not hear the next-to-last letter (e.g., bra*n*d, corre*c*t, poi*n*t).
    c. **Vowel sounds.** The student may have trouble saying vowels, especially short *e* and *i* (as in ten, tin).
    d. **Syllables.** The student may get syllables confused (e.g., crackerfire, capertillar, multicabation).
    e. **Spelling.** The student may have trouble hearing all the sounds or may put them in the wrong order. Learning words in context or in word families should help.

An Instructional Design for Dyslexic Readers

Teachers are often concerned about students who appear to be above average in intelligence but still cannot follow simple directions. For example, upper elementary and secondary students may leave homework in their desks or turn in incomplete homework. Parents of children with dyslexia frequently express frustration with the teachers: the parents are aware that their children are trying very hard to complete all assignments but struggle to complete teacher-made tests or respond to writing prompts and word problems.

Frequently, dyslexic children suffer in the regular classroom. When the educator doesn't understand the student's learning process, he or she may see the student as developmentally slow and/or unmotivated. These misconceptions may cause the dyslexic student to have low self-esteem. Once the educator understands the dyslexic student and the student's learning process, there are some ways to help the dyslexic student in the classroom.

To teach struggling readers about different elements of literature, have them read children's books to kindergarten classes. Before presenting the book, have a book discussion about the key element you want them to master or note in the books read. Below are books that teachers have classified to help struggling readers focus on specific reading concepts, ranging from nursery rhymes to story elements.

Identifying Word Families
Word families can be identified in the following nursery rhymes:
"The Northwind Doth Blow": ow, blow, snow; ing, wing thing.
"Old Mother Hubbard": ead, bread, dead; at, cat, hat; ig, wig, jig; at, oat, coat, goat
"One, Two, Buckle My Shoe": en, ten, hen; elve, twelve, delve
"One, Two, Three, Four, Five": ive, jive, five
"Peter, Peter, Pumpkin Eater": ell, shell, well
"Rain, Rain, Go Away": ay, away, day
"Rub-a-Dub-Dub": ub, dub, tub; ee, be, three
"See Saw Marjorie Daw": aw, daw, saw, straw
"Sing a Song of Sixpence": ing, king, sing; oney, money, honey
"Star Light, Star Bright": ight, light, bright, night
"Ten Little Monkeys": ed, bed, head
"There Was a Crooked Man": ile, mile, stile; ouse, mouse, house
"There Was an Old Lady Who Swallowed a Fly": at, cat, that; og, hog, dog; ow, cow, how
"Three Blind Mice": ife, wife, knife
"Three Little Kittens": en, kitten, mitten; ear, dear, fear
"This Little Piggy": ig, pig; jig; og, hog, jog
"Tom, Tom, the Piper's Son": ea, eat, beat
"Tommy Tittlemouse": ouse, Tittlemouse, house
"Tweedle-Dum and Tweedle-Dee": attle, battle, rattle
"Vintery, Mintery, Cutery, Corn": om, corn, thorn; ock, lock, flock; est, west, nest
"Wee Willie Winkie": own, town, nightgown; ock, lock, o'clock
"What Are Little Girls Made Of? What Are Little Boys Made Of?": ice, spice, nice; ails, snails, tails

"Yankee Doodle": andy, dandy, handy; ing, gooding, pudding
See also www.enchantedlearning.comlrhymeslwordfamiliesf.

- **Use of Descriptions**
  The Black Stallion, by Walter Farley
  Cloudy with a Chance of Meatballs, by Judi Barrett
  My Side of the Mountain, by Jean Craighead George
  Like Jake and Me, by Mavis Jukes
- **Use a Sound**
  Bridge to Terabithia, by Katherine Patterson
  Stone Fox, by John Reynolds Gardiner
  Zeely, by Virginia Hamilton
  In the Small, Small Pond, by Denise Fleming
- **Begin with Dialogue**
  Arthur's First Sleepover, by Marc Brown
  The Day Jimmy's Boa Ate the Wash, by Trinka Hakes Noble
  King Bidgood's in the Bathtub, by Audrey Wood
- **Start with a Question**
  Charlotte's Web, by E. B. White *Chester, the Worldly Pig*, by Bill Peet
  Shoes from Grandpa, by Mem Fox
- **Start with Action**
  Alexander and the Terrible, Horrible, No Good, Very Bad Day, by J. Viorst
- **Start with a Description**
  The Best Christmas Pageant Ever, by B. Robinson
  The Indian in the Cupboard, by L. Banks
- **Begin with a Quote**
  The Seashore Book, by Charlotte Zolotwo

Instructional Templates, Assessments, and Activities

Exhibit RS.5: Story Analysis and Language Arts: Word Sort
Story: Examine and discuss the words listed below. Group the words into categories so the words in each category share common elements. Your group should be able to explain your categories and justify your reasons for including the words in each category.

Adapted from Janet Allen, *Inside Words: Tools for Teaching Academic Vocabulary* (New York: Stenhouse Publishers, 2007).

Exhibit RS.6: Rubric
Rubrics are sets of scoring guidelines that assist teachers and students in rating the elements of a performance or project according to specific criteria. A rubric contains a point scale as well as descriptive criteria for each level of performance on a continuum of quality. The criteria are conditions that define the task requirements. The number of categories may vary according to subject, standards addressed within the unit plan, and grade level.

Below is a sample rubric that can be used for any type of writing.

An Evaluation Form for Writing

Name_____

Date_____

Scale 1-7

7= Outstanding (A)   5= Above average (B)   4= Average (C)   3=Below Average (D)   2-1=Needs Improvement (F)

_____PURPOSE (clear audience, subject, and genre)
_____DIRECTION (proper structure, organization, logical order)
_____IDEAS (connection to reader, specific details, variety)
_____STYLE (expression, word choice, sentence variety, figurative language, etc...)
_____PRESENTATION (spelling, punctuation, capitalization, paragraphing, neatness, pen or typed)

Total Score _____

GRADE _____

Instructional Resources: Books Written to Explain
I Was So Mad, by Mercer Mayer
My Dad Is Awesome, by Nick Butterworth
A Tree Is Nice, by Janice May Udry
What Makes My Mommy Best?, by Burtoil Art
I Love My Daddy Because..., by Laurel Porter-Gaylord

RESOURCE SECTION

Instructional Resources: Books Written to Inform
The Cloud Book, by Tommie de Paola
What Feet Can Do, by Elizabeth A. Thorn and Joan Irwin
Mighty Spiders, by Fay Robinson
Snow Is Falling, by Franklyn Branley
Appalachia: The Voices of Sleeping Birds, by Cynthia Rylant

Instructional Resources: Books Illustrating Varied Beginnings
    The Gold Coin, by Alma Florada
    The True Story of the Three Little Pigs! by A. Wolf, by Jon Scieszka
    Tuck Triumphant, by Theodore Taylor

Instructional Resources: Books That Reveal Family Culture Relationships and Values
    He's Got the Whole World in His Hands, by Kadir Nelson
    Barack, by Jonah Winter
    The Talking Eggs, by Robert D. San Souci
    The Little Tree Growin' in the Shade, by Camille Yarbrough
    Shortcut, by Donald Crews
    Uncle Jed's Barbershop, by Margaree King Mitchell

Instructional Resources: Books That Illustrate Elements of Writing
    Aunt Isabel Tells a Good One, by Kate Duke
    Nothing Ever Happens on 90th Street, by Rom Schotter

Instructional Resources: Books with Distinct Purposes
Distinct Settings
    Where the Forest Meets the Sea, by Jeannie Baker
    The Great Kapok Tree, by Lynne Cherry
    Miss Rumphius, by Barbara Cooney
    The Tunnel, by Anthony Browne
    Sarah, Plain and Tall, by Patricia MacLachlan
    Owl Moon, by Jane Yolen
    Mufaro's Beautiful Daughters, by John Steptoe
    When I Was Young in the Mountains, by Cynthia Tylant

The Year of the Perfect Christmas Tree, by Gloria Houston
Where the River Begins, by Thomas Locker
Three Days on a River in a Red Canoe, by Vera B. Williams
The Beach Before Breakfast, by Maxine Kumin

Reword the Beginning
My Mama Had a Dancing Heart, by Libba Moore Gray

Advise the Reader
How Smudge Came, by Nan Gregory
Mike Mulligan and His Steam Shovel, by Virginia Lee Burton

Books for Grades Three and Up Illustrating Strong Voice
The Pain and the Great One, by Judy Blume
Goodbye Geese, by Nancy Carlstrom
On the Day You Were Born, by Debra Frasier *Tight Times*, by Barbara Shooken
I Am the Ocean, by Suzanna Marshak
White Dynamite and the Curly Kid, by Bill Martin Jr. and John Archambault
Knots on a Counting Rope, by Bill Martin Jr. and John Archambault
The Relatives Came, by CyIithia Rylant
When I Was Young in the Mountains, by Cynthia Rylant
The True Story of the Three Little Pigs, by John   Scieszka *Gila Monsters Meet You at the Airport*, by Marjorie Sharmat *Stevie My Special Best Words*, by John Steptoe
Ox-Cart Man, by Donald Hall
How Much is a Million?, by David Schwartz
The River Ran Wild, by Lynne Cherry
The Great Kapok Tree, by Lynne Cherry
The Popcorn Book, by Tomi de Paola
The Prairie Boy's Winter, by William Kurelek

Books with Strong Characters
The Two of Them, by Aliki
The Song and Dance Man, by Dan Karen Ackell
Granpa, by John Burningham
My Mother's House, My Father's House, by C. B. Christiansen
Molly's Pilgrim, by Barbara Cohen
Miss Rumphius, by Barbara Cooney
Rosalie, by Jean Hewett
Through Grandpa's Eyes, by Patricia MacLachlan

Crow Boy, by Taro Yashima
Hey Al, by Arthur Yorinks
Bunicula, by Deborah and James Howe

Books Illustrating Varied Endings
End with a Feeling
I Love You the Purplest, by Barbara Joosse
Peter's Move, by Alexander James

End with a Quote
Amazing Grace, by Mary Hoffinan
The Boy Who Wouldn't Go to Bed, by Helen Cooper

Surprise Endings
Just Like Daddy, by Frank Asch
The Wednesday Surprise, by Eve Bunting
Just Like Everyone Else, by Karla Kuskin
Flossie and the Fox, by Patricia McKissack
In the Attic, by Hiawyn Oram
Super Dooper
Jezebel, by Tony Ross
The Frog Prince, by John Scieszka
Benjamin's Book, by A. Baker
Ask Mr. Bear, by M. Flack
Good Night Owl, by P. Hutchins

Circular Endings
Very Last First Time, by Jan Andrews
Grandfather Twilight, by Barbara Berger
If You Give a Mouse a Cookie, by Laura Numeroff
The Relatives Came, by Cynthia Rylant
Two Bad Ants, by Chris Van Allsburg
Louis the Fish, by Arthur Yorinks

Poignant Endings
A Father Like That, by Charlotte Zolotwo *William's Doll*, by Charlotte ctional Zolotwo
Bridge to Terabithia, by Katherine Patterson
The Children We Remember, by Chana Byers Abells
Dear Daddy, by Phyllipe Dupasquier

Wilfred Gordon McDonald Partridge, by Mem Fox
The Keeping Quilt, by Patricia Polacco
The Year of the Perfect Christmas Tree, by Barbara Houston

End with a Question
Grandpa's Song, by Tony Johnston
Shoes from Grandpa, by Mem Fox
Which Witch Is Which, by Pat Hutchins

GLOSSARY OF SELECT TERMS

Accommodation: a procedure to adjust a situation to solve a problem. For example, in the classroom, a struggling dyslexic reader may be accommodated by recording oral responses to a story rather than by requiring written responses.

Accountability: To be responsible for an action or behavior to affect change or expectations.

Administrative leader: The person in charge of an institution or agency.

Alternative Assessment: An act or procedure used to measure the real ability and achievement of a student other than through the usual paper and pencil multiple-choice tests (Examples are projects, portfolios, interviews).

Comprehension: the skill of being able to visualize what is read and bring meaning to the printed word through prior knowledge, vicarious or actual experiences.

Dyslexia: a learning difference that is caused by inherited neurological brain functions that affect the way one perceives language (visual, auditory, spatial, and linguistic).

Fluency: the smooth flow with which one reads; it helps to bridge meaning between decoding and comprehension.

Homograph: two or more words that have the same spelling but differ in origin, meaning, and sometimes pronunciation (e.g., band (a group of musicians), band, (a head or wrist band); tear, tear).

Homonyms: families of words that may have the same sound and spelling but different meanings (band, band); the same spelling but different sounds and meanings (tear, tear); or the same sound but different spellings and meanings (hair, hare; to, two, too).

Homophone: two words that have the same sound (phone) but have different spellings and different meanings (bear, bare; mail, male).

Idiom: a figure of speech used to paint a mental image. For example, "As easy as pie" means it was very easy. (See website by Dennis Oliver (2007), "ESL Idioms," for extensive examples and practice. Struggling readers have difficulty with this kind of abstract visualization.)

Modifying: the process of changing a given situation or thing. In education, it is similar to making accommodations—creating a different way for an assignment to be completed while reaching the same overall lesson objective.

Multisyllabic words: words that have two or more syllables. Occasionally a word has a cluster of consonants in the middle. To pronounce this type of word, keep the two letters together that make a team, such as the *th* in athlete.

Onset: the letters at the beginning of words or syllables up to the vowel but not including the vowel (e.g., *fr* in frog).

Phoneme: a speech sound; the smallest unit of sound that makes a difference in meaning.

Phonemic awareness: the conscious understanding that spoken language is composed of speech sounds (phonemes). It involves the ability to hear and duplicate sounds as related to words and accurately apply letter sounds in words.

Phonics: the study of relationships between spoken sounds and their written alphabetic symbols.

Phonological awareness: a comprehensive term that includes phonemic awareness and the manipulation of phonemes in spoken and written words.

Progress monitoring: an ongoing process that may be measured through informal classroom assessment, benchmark assessment instruments, and/or large-scale assessments (e.g., district or state tests).

Reading disability: the inability to read as peers at the expected level even though the student has been exposed to the same quality instruction.

Reciprocal Teaching: the instructional process that incorporates the reading strategies of predicting, questioning, clarifying, and summarizing.

Response to Intervention (RtI): the tiered integration of assessments and interventions designed for progress monitoring, including the strengths and growth as a result of individualized focus within a time frame and academic goal setting based on student needs.

GLOSSARY OF SELECT TERMS

Rimes: the vowel and all the letters that follow it in a word (e.g., *end* in blend). Most syllables have a rime, but may not have onsets as in two-letter words (e.g., at, of). (See definition for onset.)

Rubrics: sets of scoring guidelines that assist teachers and students in rating the elements of a performance or project according to specific criteria.

Tier 1: quality classroom instruction based on a standard curriculum framework.

Tier 2: supplemental instruction that focuses on conceptual gaps assessed in Tier 1.

Tier 3: intensive interventions (usually thirty minutes to one hour daily) specifically designed to meet the individual needs of students who did not succeed in Tiers 1 and 2.

Vocabulary: words used by, understood by, or at the command of a particular person or group to communicate orally or in print.

SELECTED BIBLIOGRAPHY

Ackerman, R. H., and P. Maslin-Ostrowski. 2004. "The wounded leader." *Educational Leadership* 61(7): 28–32.

Adams, G., and S. Brown. 2004. *The six-minute solution: A reading fluency program; Grades 3–8 and remedial high school.* Longmont, CO: Sopris West Educational Services.

Allen, J. 2007. *Inside Words: Tools for teaching academic vocabulary.* New York: Stenhouse Publishers.

Allen, L. M. 1996. *Administrators' perceptions of the effectiveness of reading recovery as an early literacy intervention program for at-risk first graders* (Unpublished doctoral dissertation). Jackson, MS: Jackson State University.

Allen, N. M. 2012. *When teaching gets tough: Smart ways to reclaim your game.* Alexandria, VA: ASCD.

Allington, R. A., and S. Walmsey, Eds. 2007. *No quick fix, the RTI edition: Rethinking literacy programs in America's elementary schools.* New York: Teacher's College Press.

Allington, R. L. 2001. "The reading instruction provided readers of differing abilities." *Elementary School Journal* 83: 548–559.

———. 2004. "Setting the record straight: Federal officials are holding schools to impossible standards based on misinterpretations of research." *Educational Leadership* 61(5): 22–25.

———. 2000, 2001. *What really matters for struggling readers.* New York: Addison Wesley Longman.

Allington, R. L., and K. Baker. 1999. *Best practices in literacy instruction for children with special needs. Best Practices in Literacy Instruction* (4th ed.). New York: Guilford Press.

Allor, J., and R. McCathren. 2004. "The efficacy of an early literacy tutoring program Implemented by college students." *Learning Disabilities Research & Practice* 19(2): 116–129.

SELECTED BIBLIOGRAPHY

Anderson, V., and M. Roit. 2001. "Reading as a gateway to language proficiency for language-minority students in the early grades." *Reading research anthology*, the Consortium of Reading Excellence. Novato, CA: Arena Press. (Originally from *Promoting learning for culturally and linguistically diverse students: Classroom applications from contemporary research*, 1998).

Archer, A. L., M. M. Gleason, and V. Vachon. 2005. *Reading excellence: Word attack & rate development strategies (REWARDS)*.Longmont, CO: Sopris West Educational Services.

Barton, S. 2008. *Teaching people with dyslexia*. Retrieved from http://www.barton-reading.com/.

Battisbone, A. 2004. *Map your thinking*. Cary, NC: Thinking Maps.

Bauman, J., and E. Kame'enui, eds. 2004. *Vocabulary instruction: Research to practice*. New York: Guilford Press.

Bean, R. M. 2004a. "Promoting effective literacy instruction: The challenge for literacy coaches." *The California Reader* 37(3): 58–63.

———. 2004b. *The reading specialist: Leadership for the classroom, school, and community*. New York: Guilford Press.

Bean, R. M., A. L. Swan, and R. Kanab. 2003. Reading specialists in schools with exemplary reading programs: Functional, versatile, and prepared. *The Reading Teacher* 54(5): 446–455.

Beck, I. 2006. *Making sense of phonics*. New York: Guilford Press.

Beck, I., and M. McKeown. 2005. *Text talk: Levels A & B*. New York: Scholastic.

Beck, I., M. McKeown, and L. Kukan. 2002. *Bringing words to life: Robust vocabulary instruction*. New York: Guilford Press.

Beck, I. L., and C. Juel. 2001. "The role of decoding in learning to read." In *Reading research anthology: The why? of reading instruction*, 2nd ed., edited by L. Gutlohn, L. Diamond, and B. J. Thorsnes, 52–61. Novato, CA: Arena Press.

Ben-Yodel, E. 2003. "Respecting students' cultural literacies." *Educational Leadership* 61(2): 80–82.

Bereiter, C., A. Brown, J. Campione, I. Carruthers, R. Case, J. Hirshberg, M. J. Adams, A. McKeough, M. Pressley, M. Roit, M. Scardamalia, and G. H. Treadway. 2000/2002. *Open court reading*. (Grades K–6 reading and writing program.) Columbus, OH: SRA/McGraw-Hill.

Birsh, J. R. (2011). Connecting research and practice. In J. R. Birsh, *Multisensory teaching of basic language skills* (3rd ed., pp. 1–24). Baltimore, MD: Paul H. Brookes Publishing.

Blachman, B. A., C. Schatschneider, J. M. Fletcher, D. J. Francis, S. M. Clonan, B. A. Shaywitz, and S. E. Shaywitz. 2004. "Effects of intensive reading remediation for second and third grades and a 1-year follow-up." *Journal of Educational Psychology* 96(3): 444–461.

Blanchard, K., S. Bowles, D. Carew, and E. Parisi-Carew. 2001. *High five: The magic of working together*. New York: Harper Collins.

Blum, I. H., and P. S. Koskinen. 2001. "Repeated reading: A strategy for enhancing fluency and fostering expertise." Gutlohn, L., L. Diamond, and B. J. Thorsnes (Eds.), *Reading research anthology: The why? of reading instruction* (2nd ed.). Novato, CA: Arena Press.

Boykin, A. W., & Bailey, C.T. (2000). The role of cultural factors in school relevant cognitive functioning: Synthesis of findings on cultural context, cultural orientations, and individual differences. (ERIC Document Reproduction Service No. ED 441 880).

Bromley, K. 2002. *Stretching students' vocabulary, 3–8*. New York: Scholastic.

Brooks, J. D. 1991. "Teaching to identified learning styles: The effects upon oral and silent reading and listening comprehension." PhD diss., University of Toledo, Ohio.

Broomfield, H., and M. Combley. 1997. *Overcoming dyslexia: A practical handbook for the classroom* (2nd ed.). Philadelphia: Whurr Publishers.

Brown, I. S., and R. H. Felton. 1990. "Effects of instruction on beginning reading skills in children at risk for reading disability." *Reading and Writing: An Interdisciplinary Journal* 2: 223–241.

Brown, K., D. Morris, and M. Fields. 2005. "Intervention after grade 1: Serving increased numbers of struggling readers effectively." *Journal of Literacy Research* 37(1): 61–94.

Brulle, A. 2005. "What can you say when research and policy collide?" *Phi Delta Kappa* 86(6): 433–437.

Burroughs-Lange, S. 2007. *Evaluation of Reading Recovery in London schools: Every child a reader 2005–2006*. University of London, Department for Education and Skills Departmental Report 2007, TSO (The Stationery Office). Retrieved from www.dcsf.gov.uk/aboutus/reports/pdfs/deptreport2007.pdf.

Burroughs-Lange, S., and J. Douetil. 2007. Literacy progress of young children from poor urban settings: A Reading Recovery comparison study. *Literacy Teaching and Learning* 12(1): 19–46.

Caine, R. N., G. Caine, C. McClintic, and K. J. Klimek. 2009. *12 Brain/mind learning principles in action, developing executive functions of the human brain*. 2nd ed. Thousand Oaks, CA: Corwin Press.

Camilli, G., S. Vargas, and M. Yurecko. 2004. "Teaching children to read: The fragile link between science and federal education policy." *Education Policy Analysis Archives* (EPAA) abstracted from *Current Index to Journals in Education*.

Campbell, L., and C. Kelly. 2004. "Helping struggling readers." *New Horizons for Learning*. Retrieved from http://education.jhu.edu/PD/newhorizons/strategies/topics/literacy/articles/helping-struggling-readers.

Carbo, M., 2007. Becoming a great teacher of reading: Achieving high, rapid reading gains with powerful differentiated strategies. Thousand Oaks, Calif.: Corwin Press and the National Association of Elementary School Principals.

Carlisle, J., and M. Rice. 2002. *Improving reading comprehension*. Timonium, MD: York Press.

Carnegie Mellon University. 2008. "Remedial instruction can make strong readers out of poor readers, brain imaging study reveals." Retrieved from www.sciencedaily.com/releases/2008/06/080611103900.htm.

———. 2008. "Remedial instruction rewires dyslexic brains, provides lasting results, study shows." *Science Daily*, August 7. Retrieved from www.sciencedaily.com/releases/2008/08/0808055124056.htm.

Chall, J. 1998. *Learning to read: The great debate.* New York: McGraw-Hill.

Chall, J., and V. A. Jacobs. 2003. The classic study on poor children's fourth grade slump. *American Educator* 27(l): 14–44. Washington, DC: American Federation of Teachers.

Chard, D., M. Coyne, L. Edwards, R. Good, B. Harn, E. Kame'enui, and D. Simmons. 2004. *Big ideas in beginning reading.* Retrieved from the University of Oregon website: http//reading.uoregon.edu.

Chenoweth, T. G., and R. B. Everhart. 2002. *Navigating comprehensive school change.* New York: Eye on Education Publications.

Clay, M. 2002. *An observation survey for early literacy achievement.* 2nd ed. Portsmouth, NH: Heineman

———. 1991. *Becoming literate.* Portsmouth, NH: Heineman Education Division.

———. 1998. *By different paths to common outcomes.* York, MD: Stenhouse. Improving performance and narrowing the equity gap. Retrieved from www.coreknowledge.org/Ckkproto2/about/eval/EvalPktRpt.htm.

Compton, G. 1992. "The reading connection: A leadership initiative designed to change the delivery of educational services to at-risk children." Unpublished doctoral dissertation, Kalamazoo: Western Michigan University.

Cooper, B., and M. Pislochini. 1998. *Stopping reading failure: Reading intervention for intermediate grade students.* New York: Houghton Mifflin.

Cooter, R. B. 2003. "Teacher 'capacity-building' helps urban children succeed in reading." *The Reading Teacher* 57(2): 198–205.

CORE (Consortium of Reading Excellence). 2001. *Teaching reading sourcebook*. Novato, CA: Arena Press.

Cornwell L. 2015. Retrieved from http://www.scholastic.com/librarians/programs/whatisrt.com

Crockett, W.L. 2004. Inbounds: Cognitive-behavioral counseling model for adolescent males in middle school. Unpublished Post Doctoral Paper.

Crockett, M.B. 2005. Accountability and perceptions of elementary school administrators in the literacy instruction of struggling readers . Unpublished Dissertation.

Cunningham, A. E., and K. E. Stanovich. 1997. "Early reading acquisition and its relation to reading experience and ability 10 years later." *Developmental Psychology* 33: 934–945.

Cunningham, P. 1998. *Four reading blocks* (videotape). Washington, DC: National Reading Panel, US Department of Education.

Cunningham, W. G., and P. A. Cordeiro. 2000. *Educational administration: A problem-based approach*. Boston: Allyn and Bacon.

D'Arcangelo, M. 1999. "Learning about learning to read: A conversation with Sally Shaywitz." *Educational Leadership* 57: 26–31.

Dean, C. B., E. R. Hubbell, H. Pitler, and B. Stone. 2012. *Classroom instruction that works*. 2nd ed. Denver, CO: McREL (Mid-continent Research for Education and Learning).

Delpit. L. 1995. *Other people's children: Cultural conflict in the classroom*. New York: New Press.

Diamond, L., and L. Gutlohn. 2006. CORE *literacy library: Vocabulary handbook*. Berkeley, CA: CORE.

Dorn, L. J., C. French, and T. Jones. 1998. *Apprenticeship in literacy*. New York: Stenhouse Publishers.

Dougherty, E. 2012. *Assignments matter: Making the connection that help students meet standards*. Alexandria, VA: ASCD.

Doyle, J. 2005. *Phonemic awareness, phonics, and fluency*. Paper presented at the FCRR SLP Reading Academy, Tallahassee, FL.

Ehri, L., L. Dreyer, B. Flugman, and A. Gross. 2007. "Reading rescue: An effective tutoring intervention model for language-minority students who are struggling readers in first grade." *American Educational Research Journal* 44(2): 414–448.

Eide, D. 2011. *Uncovering the logic of English: A common-sense solution to America's literacy crisis*. Minneapolis, MN: Pedia Learning.

Eiter, M. 2002. "Best practices in leadership development, lessons from the best business Schools and corporate universities." In *The principal challenge*, edited by M. S. Tucker and L. Coddig, 99–122. San Francisco: Jossey-Bass.

Elbaum, B., S. Baughn, M. T. Hughes, and S. W. Moody. 2000. "How effective are one-to-one tutoring programs in reading for elementary students at risk for reading failure? A meta-analysis of the intervention research." *Journal of Educational Psychology* 92: 605–619.

Erlauer, L. 2003. *The brain-compatible classroom: Using what we know about learning to improve teaching*. Alexandria, VA: Association for Supervision and Curriculum Development (ASCD).

Fischman, J. 2001. "New reading programs spell help for frustrated kids." *U.S. News & World Report* 130(15): 48–53.

Fisher, D., and N. Frey. 2010. *Guided instruction, How to develop confident and successful learners*. Alexandria, VA: ASCD.

Florida Center for Reading Research. 2005. *Teacher resource guide: K–1 student center activities*. Tallahassee, FL.

Florida Department of Education. 2006. *Sunshine state standards: K–12 reading and language arts*. Retrieved from http://etc.usf.edu/flstandards/la/la_sss.pdf.

Foorman, B.R., & Santi, K.L. (2004). The teaching of reading. In L.J. Saha and A.G. Dworkin (Eds.), The New International Handbook of Teachers and Teaching. Norwell, MA: Springer.

Foorman, B., D. Francis, J. Fletcher, C. Scatschneider, and P. Mehta. 1998. "The role of instruction in learning to read: Preventing reading failure in at-risk children." *Journal of Education Psychology* 90(I): 37–55.

Foorman, B. R., D. J. Grancis, D. Winikates, P. Mehta, C. Schatschneider, and J. M. Fletcher. 1997. "Early interventions for children with reading disabilities." *Scientific Studies of Reading* 1: 255–276.

Fountas, I. C., and G. S. Pinnell. 1999. *Matching books to readers: Using leveled books in guided reading, K–3*. Portsmouth, NH: Heinemann.

Fry, E. B. 2004. *The vocabulary teacher's book of lists*. San Francisco: Jossey-Bass Books.

Fuchs, D., and L. S. Fuch. 2006. "Introduction to response to intervention: What, why, and how valid is it?" *Reading Research Quarterly* 41(1): 92–128.

Fukkink, R. G., and K. de Clopper. 1998. "Effects of instruction in deriving word meaning from context: A meta-analysis." *Review of Educational Research* 68(4): 450–469.

Fullan, M. 1999. *Change forces: The sequel*. Bristol, PA: Falmer Press.

Fullan, M. G. (1994). Teacher leadership: A failure to conceptualize. In D. R. Walling (Ed.), Teachers as leaders (pp. 241 -253). Bloomington, IN: Phi Delta Kappa Educational Foundation..

Futrell, M. H. 1999. "Empowering teachers as learners and leaders." In *Readings on leadership in Education*, 125–141. Bloomington, IN: Phi Delta Kappan Foundation.

Gambrell, L. B., L. M. Morrow, S. B. Neuman, and M. Pressley. 1999. *Best practices in literacy instruction*. New York: Guildford Press.

Gardner, H. 1999. *Intelligence reframed: Multiple intelligences for the 21st century*. New York: Basil Books.

Gersten, R., D. Compton, C. Connor, J. Cimino, L. Santoro, S. Linan-Thompson, and W. Tilly. 2009. *Assisting students struggling with reading: Response to intervention and multitier intervention in the primary grades. A practice guide*. (NCEE 2009-4045). Washington, DC: National Center for Education Evaluation and Regional Assistance, Institute of Education Sciences, US Department of Education. Retrieved from http://ies.ed.gov/ncee/wwc/publications/practiceguides.

Glaser, D., and L. C. Moats. 2008. *Foundations LETRS: An introduction to language and literacy*. Boston: Sopris West Educational Services.

Goldberg, M. 2000. *Profiles of leadership in education*. Bloomington, IN: Phi Delta Kappa Educational Foundation, pp. 62-67

———. 2005. "Test mess 2: Are we doing better a year later?" *Phi Delta Kappan* 86(5): 389–395.

Goldstein, L. 2004. "Highly qualified? Teaching students with disabilities to high standards will depend on the skills of their teachers." *Education Week* 23(17).

Good, R. H., R. A. Kaminski, S. Smith, E. Kame'enui, and J. Wallin. 2003. "Reviewing outcomes: Using DIBELS to evaluate kindergarten curricula and interventions." In *Reading in the classroom: Systems for the observation of teaching and learning*, edited by S. Vaughn and K. Briggs, 221–259. Baltimore, MD: Brooks Publishing.

Good III, R. H., D. C. Simmons, and S. B. Smith. 2001. "Effective academic interventions in the United States: Evaluating and enhancing the acquisition of early reading skills." In *Reading research anthology: The why? of reading instruction*, 2nd ed., edited by L. Gutlohn, L. Diamond, and B. J. Thorsnes, 218–230. Novato, CA: Arena Press.

Gorman, C. 2003. "The new science of dyslexia." *Time* 162(4), 52–59.

Graseck, P. 2005. "Where's the ministry in administration?" *Phi Delta Kappan* 86(5): 373–377.

Graves, M. 2006. *The vocabulary book: Learning and instruction*. New York: Teachers College Press.

Gronlund, N. 2003. *Assessment of student achievement*. Boston: Allyn and Bacon.

Grossen, B. 1997. *Thirty years of research: What we know about how children learn to read: A synthesis of research on reading from the National Institute of Child Health and*

Human Development. Santa Cruz, CA: The Center for the Future of Teaching and Learning.

Gunn, B., K. Smolkowski, A. Biglan, and C. Black. 2002. "Supplemental instruction in decoding skills for Hispanic and Non-Hispanic students in early elementary school: A follow up." *Journal of Special Education* 36(2): 69–79.

Gutlohn, L., L. Diamond, and B. J. Thorsnes, eds. 2001. *Reading research anthology: The why? of reading instruction.* 2nd ed. Novato, CA: Arena Press.

Harari, O. 2002. *The leadership secrets of Colin Powell.* New York: McGraw-Hill.

Hargreaves, A., and M. Fullan, M. 1998. *What's worth fighting for out there?* New York: Teachers College Press.

Harvey S., and A. Goudvis. 2000. *Strategies that work: Teaching comprehension to enhance understanding.* Markham, Ontario: Pembroke Publishers.

Hatcher, P. J., K. Goetz, M. J. Snowling, C. I. Hulme, S. Gibbs, and G. Smith. 2006. "Evidence of effectiveness of the early literacy support programme." *British Journal of Educational Psychology* 76: 351–367.

Hatcher, P. J., C. Hulme, and A. W. Ellis. 1994. "Ameliorating early reading failure by integrating the teaching of reading and phonological skills: The phonological linkage hypothesis." *Child Development* 65: 41–57.

Honig, B., L. Diamond, and L. Gutlohn. 2001. *Teaching reading*: Sourcebook for kindergarten through eighth grade. Novato, CA: Arena Press.

———. 2004. *CORE: Teaching reading sourcebook.* Novato, CA: Arena Press.

Huggins, R. 1999. *Longitudinal study of the Reading Recovery program, 1994–1998.* Detroit: Detroit Public Schools, Office of Research, Evaluation and Assessment.

Hurford, D. M. 1998. *To read or not to read.* New York: A Lisa Drew Book/Scribner.

Hurry, J., and K. Sylva. 2007. "Long-term outcomes of early reading intervention." *Journal of Research in Reading* 30(3): 227–248.

Hyerle, D., and C. Yeager. 2007. *Thinking maps: A language for learning.* Cary, NC: Innovative Sciences.

International Dyslexia Association. 2003. "Mathematics, [reading] and dyslexia." *Online Perspectives*. Retrieved from www.Idonline.org/Id_indepth/math.

International Reading Association. 2003. *Standards for reading professionals*. Newark, DE: Author.

International Reading Association. 2000. "Teaching all children to read: The roles of the reading specialist. A position statement of the International Reading Association., Newark, NJ: Author.

Jenkins, J. R., J. A. Peyton, E. A. Sanders, and P. F. Vadasy. 2004. "Effects of reading decodable texts in supplemental first-grade tutoring." *Scientific Studies of Reading* 8: 53–85.

Jensen, E. 2000. *Different brains, different learners: How to reach the hard to reach*. Thousand Oaks, CA: Corwin Press.

Johnson, D. W., and R. T. Johnson. 1999. *Learning together and alone: Cooperative, competitive and individualistic learning*. 5th ed. Boston: Allyn and Bacon.

Johnson, D. W., G. I. Maruyama, R. T. Johnson, D. Nelson, and L. Skon. 1981. "Effects of cooperative, competitive and individualistic goal structures on achievement: A meta-analysis." *Psychological Bulletin* 89: 47–62. Boston: Allyn and Bacon.

Johnson, J. 2004. "What school leaders want." *Educational Leadership* 61(7): 24–27.

———. 1991. *Caring n' sharing (preventive counseling)*. 3rd edition. Madison, MS: The Johnson Ministries.

Johnson-Gross, K. N. 2008. "Response to intervention (RtI)." PowerPoint presentation. Jackson: Mississippi Department of Education.

John Hopkins University, School of Ed/USDE. n.d. Online report. *Best Evidence Encyclopedia*. Retrieved from www.bestevidence.org.

Joshi, M. J., M. Dahlgren, and R. Boulware-Gooden. 2002. "Teaching reading in an inner city school through a multisensory teaching approach." *Annals of Dyslexia* 52. Baltimore, MD: The Orton Dyslexia Society.

Juel, C. 2001. "What kind of tutoring helps a poor reader?" In *Reading research anthology: The why? of reading instruction*. Novato, CA: Arena Press.

Kame'enui, E. J. 2001. "Diverse learners and the tyranny of time: Don't fix blame; fix the leaky roof." In *Reading research anthology: The why? of reading instruction*, 210–217. Novato, CA: Arena Press.

Kame'enui, E. J., D. W. Carnine, R. C. Dixon, D. C. Simmons, and M. Coyne. 2002. *Effective teaching strategies that accommodate diverse learners* 2nd ed. Columbus, OH: Merrill Prentice Hall.

Keene, E. O., and S. Zimmerman. 1997. *Mosaic of thought*. Portsmouth, NH: Heinemann.

Kelly, C., and L. Campbell. 2004. "Helping struggling readers." Retrieved from www.Nehorizons.Org/epneeds/inclusion/teaching/kelly.htm.

Kerper, M. J. 2002. *A phonics instruction sequence for CLAD reading*. Retrieved from http//coe.sdsu.edu/people/jomora/PhonicsSequence.htm.

Kindergarten and first grade teacher reading academy. 2004. Massachusetts Partnership for Achievement in Reading.

Kovalevs, K., and A. Dewsbury. 2006. *Making connections: Reading comprehension skills and strategies; Teacher's edition, book 1*. Cambridge, MA: Educators Publishing Service.

Lashway, L. 1999. "Multidimensional school leadership." In *Readings on leadership in education*, 21–50. Bloomington, IN: Phi Delta Kappa Educational Foundation.

Lehr, F., J. Osborn, and E. Heibert. 2004. "A focus on vocabulary." *Pacific Resources for Education and Learning (PREL) Monograph*. Retrieved from www.prel.org/programs/rel/vocabularyforym.asp.

Liuzzo, J. M. 2008. *A multi-sensory reading methodology: Teacher-training manual*. 3rd ed. Birmingham, MI: The Institute for Multi-Sensory Education.

Lovely, G. 2004. "Strategies for struggling readers." Retrieved from www.GailLovely.com/strugglingreaders%20readers%20resources.htm.

Lyon, G. R. 1998. "Reading: A research-based approach." In *What's gone wrong in American's classrooms?*, edited by W. M. Evers. Stanford, CA: Hoover Institution Press, pp 1-6.

———. 1999. "State of research." In *Learning disabilities: Lifelong issues*, edited by S. Cramer and W. Ellis. Baltimore, MD: Brooks Publishing, pp. 5-15

———. 2001. "Why reading is not a natural process." In *Reading research Anthology: The why? of reading instruction*, 2nd ed., edited by L. Gutlohn, L. Diamond, and B. J. Thorsnes, 6–10. Novato, CA: Arena Press.

———. 2003. *National Institute of Child Health and Human Development*. Washington, DC: National Institutes of Health.

Lyon, G. R., and V. Chhabra. 2004. "Science of reading research." *Educational Leadership* 61(6): 13–17.

Magill, K. 2003a. "Just read, Florida! Frequently asked questions about the elementary reading block." Florida Department of Education. Retrieved from http://justreadflorida.com/faq/default.asp?Cat=25.

———. 2003b. "Just read, Florida! The elementary reading block." Florida Department of Education. Retrieved from www.justreadflorida.com/90-minute-chart.asp.

Mango, K. K. 2004. "Basic measures." *Education Week* 23(17), pp. 39-41..

Marzano, R.J. (2011a). Art and science of teaching/Relating to students. It's what you do that counts. *Educational Leadership, 68*(6), 82-83.

Mathes, P. G., C. A. Denton, J. M. Fletcher, J. L. Anthony, D. J. Grancis, and C. Schatschneider. 2005. "The effects of theoretically different instruction and student characteristics on the skills of struggling readers." *Reading Research Quarterly* 40(2): 148–182.

Mathes, P. G., J. K. Howard, S. H. Allen, and D. Fuchs. 1998. "Peer-assisted learning strategies for first-grade readers: Responding to the needs of diverse learners." *Reading Research Quarterly* 33: 62–94.

McEwan, E. K. 1998. *The principal's guide to raising reading achievement*. Thousand Oaks, CA: Corwin Press.

―――. 2002. *Teach them all to read: Catching the kids who fall through the cracks.* Thousand Oaks, CA: Corwin Press.

―――. 2003. *Ten traits of highly effective principals, from good to great performance.* Thousand Oaks, CA: Corwin Press.

―――. 2004. *Seven strategies of highly effective readers, using cognitive research to boost K–8 achievement.* Thousand Oaks, CA: Corwin Press.

McGhee, M. W., and S. W. Nelson. 2005. "Sacrificing leadership, villainizing leadership: How educational accountability policies impair school leadership." *Phi Delta Kappan*, 86(5),367–372.

McGill, F. A. 1987. "Reading." *Research Quarterly* 22: 475.

―――. 2004. "Classroom leadership." *Remedial and Special Education* 12: 203. Retrieved from www.ascd.org/readingroom/classlead.

McKenna, M. C., and S. A. Stahl. 2003. *Assessment for reading instruction.* New York: Guilford Press.

McKeown, M., and I. Beck. 2004. "Direct and rich vocabulary instruction." In *Vocabulary instruction: Research to practice*, edited by J. Bauman and E. Kame'enui, 13–27. New York: Guilford Press.

Miller, D. 2002. *Reading with meaning.* Portland, ME: Stenhouse Publishers.

Mississippi Department of Education. 2009. *Mississippi dyslexia handbook: Guidelines and procedures concerning dyslexia and related disorders* (Unpublished manuscript). Jackson, MS.

Mississippi Department of Education, Office of Reading, Early Childhood & Language Arts. 2001, 2005. *Guide to research-based* reading programs. Limited Circulation (Vol. I). Jackson, MS.

Moats, L., and K. E. Dakin. 2008. *Basic facts about dyslexia & other reading problems.* Baltimore, MD: The International Dyslexia Association.

Moats, L. 2000. *Speech to print.* Baltimore, MD: Brookes Publishing.

Moats, L. C. 1999. *Teaching reading is rocket science*. Retrieved from http://aftonline.com.

Morris, D., B. Tyner, and J. Perney. 2000. "Early steps: Replicating the effects of a first-grade reading intervention program." *Journal of Educational Psychology* 92(4): 681–693.

National Assessment Governing Board. 2005. *Reading framework for the 2009 national assessment of educational progress.* US Department of Education. Retrieved from www.nagb.org/content/nagb/assets/documents/publications/frameworks/reading/2009-reading-framework.pdf.

National Assessment of Educational Progress. 2000. *The nation's report card: reading.* Washington, DC: National Center for Education Statistics.

National Assessment of Educational Progress. 2007. *The nation's report card.* Washington, DC: National Center for Education Statistics.

National Center for Educational Statistics. n.d. *Fast facts.* Washington, DC. Retrieved from http://nces.edgov/fastfacts/display.asp?id=372.

National Center for Education Statistics. 1999. *Promising results: Participation of Migrant Students in Title I Migrant Education Program.* US Department of Education and Institute of Education Sciences. Retrieved from http://nces.ed.gov/surveys/frss/publications/2000061/index.asp?sectionid=2.

National Institute of Child Health and Human Development. 2001. *Put reading first: Research building blocks for teaching children to read.* Washington, DC: Government Printing Office. Retrieved from www.nichd.nih.gov/publications/Pages/pubs_details.aspx?pubs_id=226.

National Institute of Child Health and Development. 2001. *Report of the National Reading Panel: Teaching Children to Read.* Retrieved from www.nichd.nih.gov.

National Reading Panel. 2000. *Put reading first.* Washington, DC: US Department of Education: The National Institute for Literacy.

National Reading Panel. 2000. *Teaching children to read: An evidence-based assessment of the scientific research literature on reading and its implications for reading instruction.* Rockville, MD: National Institute of Child Health and Human Development.

Neuman, S. B., and D. K. Dickinson. 2001. *Handbook of early literacy research*. New York: Guilford Press.

No Child Left Behind Mandate and News Releases. 2001, 2004. Retrieved from www.ed.gov/new/pressreleases/2004/01/01142004.html.

Oliver, D. 2007. ESL Idiom page Retrieved from http://www.eslcafe.com/idioms/id-list.html.

Orton Dyslexia Society. 1984. *Annals of Dyslexia: An Interdisciplinary Journal* 34. pp. 15-27, Baltimore, MD: The Orton Dyslexia Society.

Owens, R. 2005. *Language development: An introduction*. Boston: Pearson.

Parker, C. E., and J. Dustman. 2005. *30 Graphic organizers with lessons & transparencies*. Huntington Beach, CA: Shell Educational Publishing.

Payne, R. K. 2005. *A framework for understanding poverty*. 4th ed. Highlands, TX: Aha! Process.

Perez, K. 2008. *More than 100 brain-friendly tools and strategies for literacy instruction*. Thousand Oaks, CA: Corwin Press.

Person, D., and N. Duke. 2002. "Comprehension instruction." In *Comprehension instruction: Research-based best practices*, edited by C. C. Brock and M. Pressley, 247–258. New York: Guilford Press.

Pinnell, G. S., and I. C. Fountas. 1998. *Word matters: Teaching phonics and spelling in the reading/writing classroom*. Portsmouth, NH: Heinemann.

Pinnell, G. S., C. A. Lyons, D. E. DeFoprd, A. S. Bryk, and M. Seltzer. 1994. "Comparing instructional models for the literacy education of high-risk first graders." *Reading Research Quarterly* 29(1): 8–39.

PMRN *user's guide, version* 4.0. 2006. Tallahassee: Florida Center for Reading Research.

Polacco, P (1998). Thank you, Mr. Falker. New York, NY: Philomel Books.

Policy Exchange. 2009. "Every child a reader: An example of how top-down education reforms make matters worse." Retrieved from www.policyexchange.org.uk.

Polselli, A., and C. Snow, eds. 2003. *Rethinking reading comprehension.* New York: Guilford Press.

Portin, B. 2004. "The roles that principals play." *Educational Leadership* 61(4): 14–18.

Portland Public Schools Office of Teaching and Learning. 2006. *Pre-kindergarten benchmarks, instructional strategies, and language of instruction.* Retrieved from http://129.191.14.139/teachers.pps.k12.or.us./literacy/esliteracy/standards.html.

Pressley, M. 2000. "Comprehension instruction: What makes sense now, what might make sense soon." In *Handbook of reading research* (Vol. 3), edited by D. Pearson. Mahwah, NJ: Lawrence Erlbaum Associates.

Prince, C. D. 2002. "Attracting well-qualified teachers to struggling schools." *American Teacher* 16–21, 26(a), Retrieved from complete papers online at AASA's website *www.aasa.org/issues_and_insights/issues_dept/index.htm*.

Pullen, P., H. Lane, and M. Monaghan. 2004. "Effects of a volunteer tutoring model on the early literacy development of struggling first grade students." *Reading Research and Instruction* 43(4): 21–40.

Rasinski, T. 2003. *The fluent reader.* New York: Scholastic Professional Books.

Reeves, A. R. 2011. *Where great teaching begins, planning for student thinking and learning.* Alexander, VA: ASCD (Association of Supervision and Curriculum Development).

Reutzel, D. R., and R. B. Cooter Jr. 2004. *Teaching children to read, putting the pieces together.* 4th ed. New Jersey: Pearson-Merrill Prentice Hall.

Rothstein, R. 2004. "A wider lens on the black-white achievement gap." *Phi Delta Kappan* 86(2): 105–110.

Rouse, C. E., and A. B. Krueger. 2004. "Putting computerized instruction to the test: A randomized evaluation of a 'scientifically-based' reading program." *Economics of Education Review* 23(4): 323–338.

Routman, R. 2002. *Best practices in teaching: Teaching kids to read.* Retrieved from www.microsoft.com/education/default.asp?ID=Routman.

Samuelsson, S., and I. Lundberg. 1996. "The impact of environmental factors on components of reading and dyslexia." *Annals of Dyslexia* 46. The Orton Dyslexia Society.

Santa, C. M., and T. Hoien. 1999. "An assessment of early steps: A program for early intervention of reading problems." *Reading Research Quarterly* 34: 54–79.

Sapon-Shevin, M. 2003. "Inclusion: A matter of social justice." *Educational Leadership* 61(2): 75–80.

Schlechty, P. C. 1997. *Inventing better schools: An action plan for educational reform*. San Francisco: Jossey-Bass Publishers.

———. 2002. *Working on the work*. San Francisco: Jossey-Bass Publishers.

Schwahn, C., and W. Spady. 2001. *Applying the best future-focused change strategies to education*. MA: Scarecrow Press.

Schwartz, R. M. 2005. "Literacy learning of at-risk first-grade students in the Reading Recovery early intervention." *Journal of Educational Psychology* 97(2): 257–267.

Scherer, M. 2004. "A call for powerful leaders, a conversation with Rod Paige." *Educational Leadership* 61(7): 21–23.

———. 2006. "Teaching to strengths and celebrate strengths, nurture affinities: A conversation with Mel Levine." *Educational Leadership* 64(1): 8–15.

ScienceDaily. 2013. "Brain scans may help diagnose dyslexia." Retrieved from www.sciencedaily.com/releases/2013/08/130813201424.htm.

Senechal, M. 1997. "The differential effect of storybook reading on preschoolers' acquisition of expressive and receptive vocabulary." *Journal of Child Language* 24(1): 123–138.

Senge, P. 1994, 2002. *The fifth discipline: The art and practice of the learning organization*. New York: Doubleday Dell Publishing Group.

Sergiovanni, T. J., M. Burlingame, F. S. Coombs, and P. W. Thurston, P. W. 1999. *Educational governance and administration*. New York: A Viacom Company.

Seyfarth, J. T. 1999. *The principal, the leadership for new challenges.* New York: Merrill.

Shanahan, T. 2003. "Reading." *Research Quarterly* 3: 889–908.

Shaywitz, S. 2003. *Overcoming dyslexia: A new and complete science-based program for reading problems at any level.* New York: Alfred A. Knopf.

Shaywitz, S., and B. A. Shaywitz. 2004. "Reading disability and the brain." *Educational Leadership* 61: 7–11.

Shaywitz, S. E. 1992. "Evidence that dyslexia may represent the lower tail of a normal distribution of reading ability." *New England Journal of Medicine* 326: 145–50.

Short, P. M., and J. T. Greer. 2002. *Leadership in empowered schools, themes from innovative efforts.* Columbus, OH: Merrill Prentice Hall.

Shuger, L. (2012). Teen pregnancy and high school dropout: what communities are doing to address these issues. Washington, DC: The National Campaign to Prevent Teen and Unplanned Pregnancy and America's Promise Alliance.

Simmons, D., and E. Kame'enue. 1999. *Mapping instructions to achieve instructional priorities in beginning reading: Kindergarten–grade 3.* University of Oregon, Institute for the Development of Educational Achievement.

Simonsen, S. 1996. "Identifying and teaching text structures in content area classrooms." In *Content area reading and learning: Instructional strategies*, 2nd ed., edited by D. Lapp, J. Flood, and N. Farnan.pp. 59-76, Needham Heights, MA: Allyn and Bacon.

Slavin, R. E. 1995. *Cooperative learning: Theory, research and practice.* Needham Heights, MA: Allyn and Bacon.

———. 2008. "What works?: Issues in synthesizing education program evaluations." *Educational Researcher* 37(1): 5–14.

Slavin, R. E., C. Lake, B. Chambers, A. Cheung, and S. Davis. Forthcoming. "Effective reading programs for the elementary grades." *Review of Educational Research.*

Slavin, R. E., and N. A. Madden, eds. 2009. *Two million children: Success for all.* Thousand Oaks, CA: Corwin.

Slavin, R. E., N. A. Madden, L. J. Dolan, and B. A. Wasik. 1993. *Success for all in the Baltimore City Public Schools: Year 6 report.* Baltimore, MD: Johns Hopkins University, Center for Research on Effective Schooling for Disadvantaged Students.

Slingerland, B. (2005). *Slingerland screening tests for identifying children wiht specific language disablity.* Cambridge, MA: Educator's Publishing Service, Inc.

Smith, C. B. 2001. "Logical sequence of phonics skills." Retrieved from www.indiana.edu%7Ereading/phonics/d8/grade1.html

Snow, C. 2002. *Reading for understanding: Toward a research and development program in reading comprehension.* Santa Monica, CA: Rand.

Snow, C. E., S. M. Burns, and P. Griffin. 1998. *Preventing reading difficulties in young Children.* Washington, DC: National Academy Press.

Snowball, D., and F. Balton. 1999. *Spelling K–8: Planning and teaching.* York, ME: Stenhouse.

Stahl, K., and M. McKenna. 2006. *Reading research as work.* New York: Guilford Press.

Stahl, S. A. 1999. "Vocabulary development." Cambridge, MA: Brookline Books, pp 1-4; 10-13; 27-32.

Stevens, R., P. Van Meter, J. Garner, N. Warcholak, C. Bochna, and T. Hall. 2008. "Reading and integrated literacy strategies (RAILS): An integrated approach to early reading." *Journal of Education for Students Placed at Risk* 13(44): 357–380.

Stevens, R. J., N. A. Madden, R. E. Slavin, and A. M. Farnish. 1987. "Cooperative integrated reading and composition: Two field experiments." *Reading Research Quarterly* 22: 433–454.

Strickland, K. 2005. *What's after assessment.* Portsmouth, NH: Heineman.

Swanson, H. L. 1999. "Reading research intervention for students with LD: A meta-analysis of intervention outcomes." *Journal of Learning Disabilities* 32: 504–532.

Terban, M. (2007b). In a pickle: And other funny idioms: New York: Clarion Books.

Texas Education Agency. 1998. Subchapter A in *Texas essential knowledge and skills: Chapter 110. English language arts and reading.* Austin, TX: Texas Department of Education.

Texas Reading Initiative. 2002. *Guidelines for examining phonics & word recognition programs* (Rev. ed.). Austin: Texas Education Agency. Retrieved from www.tea.state.tx.us/reading/practices/redbk3.pdf.

Thomas, D., and W. L. Bainbridge. 2002. "No Child Left Behind: Facts and fallacies." *Phi Delta Kappan* 781, 10, pp. 781-782

Torgerson, C. J., G. Brooks, and J. Hall. 2006. *A systematic review of the research literature on the use of phonics in the teaching of reading and spelling.* Research Report RR711. London: Department for Education and Skills.

Torgesen, J. K. 1998. "Catch them before they fall." *American Educator* 22(1): 32–39.

Torgesen, J. K., and P. Mathes. 1998. *What every teacher should know about phonological awareness.* Florida Department of Education, Division of Public Schools and Community Education.

———. 2001. "What every teacher should know about phonological awareness." In CORE's *Reading research anthology.* 2nd ed. 38–45. Novato, CA: Arena Press.

———. 2005. *Early interventions in reading: Teacher's edition A.* Columbus, OH: SRA/McGraw-Hill.

Torgesen, J. K., R. K. Wagner, and C. A. Rashotte. 1997. "Prevention and remediation of severe reading disabilities: Keeping the end in mind." *Scientific Studies of Reading* 1: 217–234

Torgesen, J. K., R. K. Wagner, C. A. Rashotte, J. Hetton, and P. Lindamood. 2009. *Computer assisted instruction to prevent early reading difficulties in students at risk for dyslexia: Outcomes from two instructional approaches.* Tallahassee: Florida State University.

Torgesen, J. K., R. K. Wagner, C.A., E. Rose, P. Lindamood, T. Conway, and C. Garvan. 1999. "Preventing reading failure in young children with phonological processing disabilities: Group and individual responses to instruction." *Journal of Educational Psychology* 91(4): 579–593.

Tridas, E. Q. 2007. *From ABC to ADHD: What parents should know about dyslexia and attention problems.* Baltimore, MD: The International Dyslexia Association.

Truch, S. 2004. "Comparing remedial outcomes using LIPS and phonographic: an in-depth look from a clinical perspective." The Reading Foundation. Retrieved from www.Idonline.org.

Vadasy, P. F., and E. A. Sanders. 2008. "Benefits of repeated reading intervention for low-achieving fourth- and fifth-grade students." *Remedial and Special Education* 29: 235–249.

Vadasy, P. F., S. Wayne, R. O'Connor, J. Jenkins, K. Pool, M. Firebaugh, and J. Peyton. 2005. *Sound Partners: A tutoring program in phonic-based early reading.* Longmont, CO: Sopris West Educational Services.

Valencia, S. W., and M. R. Buly. 2004. "Behind test scores: What struggling readers really need." *The Reading Teacher* 57(6): 520–525.

Vaughn, S., S. Linan-Thompson, K. Kouzekanani, D. P. Bryant, S. Dickson, and S. A. Blozis. 2003. "Reading instruction groups for students with reading difficulties." *Remedial and Special Education* 24(5): 301–315.

Walpole, S., and M. McKenna. 2007. *Differentiated reading instruction: Strategies for the primary grades.* New York: Guilford Press.

Washburn, E.K., R.M. Joshi, and E.S. Binks-Cantrell. 2011b. Teacher knowledge of basic language concepts and dsylexia. Dyslexia 17:165-183.

Wasik, B. A. 1997. "Volunteer tutoring programs: Do we know what works?" *Phi Delta Kappan* 79(4): 282–287.

Wasik, B. A., and R. E. Slavin. 1993. "Prevention early reading failure with one-to-one tutoring: A review of five programs." *Reading Research Quarterly* 28: 178–200.

Webster, W. 2000. "The high performing educational manager." In *Readings on leadership in education*, 89–107. Bloomington, IN: Phi Delta Kappa Educational Foundation.

Western Regional Reading First Technical Assistance Center. 2005. Instructional Templates. National Center for Reading First Technical Assistance Center.

What Works Clearinghouse. 2009. *Beginning reading: What Works Clearinghouse Topic Report.* Retrieved from http://ies.ed.gov/ncee/wwc.

Wikipedia. 2011. Online definitions of literacy. Wikimedia Foundation.

Wilson, B. 2010. *Wilson Fluency/Basic.* Oxford, MA: Wilson Language Training Corporation.

Willis, M. G., and J. Yuhas. 2002. "Learning styles of African American children." Unpublished presentation.

"Words that signal a text's organizational structure." 2000. Retrieved from www.somers.k12.ny.us/intranet/reading/signalwords.html.

Zgonc, Y. 1999. *Phonological awareness: The missing piece to help crack the reading code.* Eau Claire, WI: Otter Creek Institute.

SUBJECT INDEX PAGE

Subject	Page Number(s)
504 Plan	14, 17-18, 145
Accommodation	58, 159
Accountability	99
Accountability and Classroom Paraprofessionals	106
Accountability of School Administrators	100
Accountability of Teachers	101
Accommodation Checklist	67
Action Plan Outline for Building a Successful	140-142
Action Research	128-132
Action Research: Standards-Based Project	134
Actual Text Presented to a Dyslexic Student	85
Activities to Enhance Tactility, Visual Acuity, and Spatial Development	55
Activities to Improve Reading and Enlarge Vocabulary	84
Addressing Diversity in the Classroom	116
Advise the Reader	156
An Instructional Design for Dyslexic Readers	151-153
Attention Deficit Disorder (ADD)	33
Attention Deficit Hyperactive Disorder (ADHD)	33, 40
Auditory Learner's Strategies	147-148
Auditory-Linguistic behaviors	47
Benjamin Bloom's Taxonomy	110, 113
Books for Grades Three and up Illustration Stories	156
Books Illustrating Various Endings	157
Brain-compatible learning environments	1, 8
Caring Adjectives	125
Characteristics of Dyslexia	1
Checklist for Reading Styles and Related Behavioral Differences	51, 52, 53, 54
Checklist for Setting up a Brain-Compatible Learning Environment	44
Classroom Management	99
Classroom Management and Accountability	107
Classroom Organizational Tips	34-35
Common Prefixes	86
Common Suffixes that Boost Word Knowledge and Reading	87
Connecting the Five Components of Reading	78
Cooperative learning	43

Decoding Spelling Continuum with Grade-Level Expectations	87
Differentiating Instruction and Accommodating Learning Differences	65
Directions for the Blend Switch Game	56
Doubling Rule	93-94
Dyslexia	1, 3, 5
Dyslexia, ADD, and Related Behavioral and Learning Differences	39
Dyslexia: Nature or Nurture?	21
Dyslexic Reading Style and Related Reading Difficulties	16
Dyslexic Student's Description of Text	85
Dysnomia	41
Dysgraphia	41
General Instructional Strategies to Enhance Learning	71-72
Hyperlexia	42
Identifying Cooperative Groups	65-66
Identifying Reading Styles and Addressing Reading Difficulties	48
Impoverished Environments and Educational Risk Factors	28
Instructional Accountability: A-to-Z Teaching Styles and Strategies for Different Learners	102-106
Intervention Methods Effective with Young Children	42
Instructional Resources: Books with Distinct Purposes Distinct Settings	155
Instructional Resources: Books Illustrating Varied Beginnings	155
Instructional Resources: Books That Reveal Family Culture Relationships and Values	155
Instructional Resources: Books Written to Inform	154
Instructional Resources: Books That Illustrate Elements of Writing	155
Instructional Resources: Books Written to Explain	154
Introductory Steps toward Differentiating Instruction	28
Instructional Templates, Assessments, and Activities	153
Jump-Start Young Writers with Phrase Writing	82
Key Principles of the Brain and the Learning Process	9
Kinesthetic and tactile behaviors	47
Leadership	99
Learning Styles	4
Learning-Different Student	19
Learning Style Called Dyslexia	4
Literacy: The Root of Academic Success	116
Literacy Strategies for Struggling Diverse Learners	117
Look, Echo, Copy, Rewrite Spelling Strategy	95
Modifying Instruction for Hard-to-Reach Students with Reading Difficulties	67
Narrative Essay	126
Nine Dimensions to African American Culture to Enhance Learning Situations	118

No Child Left Behind Act	110, 112
Organizing the Environment	34
Pacing Guide for Capitalization, Usage, Punctuation, and Spelling (CUPS): Kindergarten and First Grade	122
Pacing Guide for Capitalization, Usage, Punctuation, and Spelling CUPS: Second and Third Grades	123
Pacing Guide For Capitalization, Usage, Punctuation, and Spelling CUPS: Fourth and Fifth Grades	124
Peer-Partner Reading Record Form to Enhance Fluency	70
Perspectives of School Administrators	10
Phonics	83
Phonemic Awareness	74, 82
Phonemic Awareness and Early Vocabulary Development	82-83
Problem-Based Learning	128, 132-136
Problem-Based Learning and Action Research	133
Reading Disability	2
Reciprocal Skills of Reading and Writing	78
Reciprocal Teaching	74
Report Writing Suggested Procedures	120-121
Resource Section	139
Reword the Beginning	156
Rubric: An Evaluation Form for Writing	154
Sample Letter: Permission to Test	143
School Reform: Where Do We Go from Here?	111
Selected Best Practices and Strategies	55
Steps in Teaching Multisyllabic Words to her Struggling Readers	86
Story Analysis and Language Arts: Word Sort	153
Strategies for Bonding with Students	38-39
Student Learning Styles and Suggested Instructional Strategies	61, 62, 63, 64
Symptoms of ADDHD	41
Teaching Tips for Problem-Based Learning	72-73
Traditional Best Practices: Revisited	94
Tips for Helping the Severely Struggling Student in the Regular Classroom	146-147
Universal Instructional Strategies for Different Learners	71
Visual Learner's Strategies	148-149
Vocabulary	83
Visual-spatial behaviors	48
Websites for Interventions and Teaching Tools	32
Website for Reading Skills and Vocabulary Development	13
Word Bank for Young Writers	80-81

Printed in Poland
by Amazon Fulfillment
Poland Sp. z o.o., Wrocław